The Neglected Child

How to Recognize, Respond, and Prevent

Ginger Welch, PhD, Laura Wilhelm, EdD, and Heather Johnson, MEd

DEDICATION

For Addy Grace—GW
For Mike, Joseph, and Allyn—LHW
For Matt and Tatum—HJJ

THE NEGLECTED CHILD

How to Recognize, Respond, and Prevent

Ginger Welch, PhD
Laura Wilhelm, EdD
Heather Johnson, MEd

Gryphon House, Inc.
Lewisville, NC

Copyright

© 2013, Ginger Welch, PhD, Laura Wilhelm, EdD, and
Heather Johnson, MEd
Published by Gryphon House, Inc.
PO Box 10, Lewisville, NC 27023
800.638.0928; 877.638.7576 (fax)
Visit us on the web at www.gryphonhouse.com.

Library of Congress Cataloging-in-Publication Data

Welch, Ginger.
 The neglected child : how to recognize, respond, and prevent / by
Ginger Welch, PhD, Laura Wilhelm, EdD, and Heather Johnson, MEd.
    pages cm
 Includes bibliographical references.
 ISBN 978-0-87659-478-0
 1. Child welfare 2. Abused children. 3. Child abuse--Prevention. 4.
Abused children--Services for. 5. Criminal behavior, Prediction of. I.
Title.
 HV713.W454 2013
 362.76--dc23
                               2013007693

Bulk Purchase

Gryphon House books are available for special premiums and sales
promotions as well as for fund-raising use. Special editions or book
excerpts also can be created to specifications. For details, contact the
Director of Marketing at Gryphon House.

Disclaimer

Gryphon House, Inc. cannot be held responsible for damage, mishap,
or injury incurred during the use of or because of activities in this
book. Appropriate and reasonable caution and adult supervision of
children involved in activities, and corresponding to the age and
capability of each child involved, are recommended at all times. Do
not leave children unattended at any time. Observe safety and
caution at all times.

ACKNOWLEDGMENTS

We gratefully acknowledge the early childhood professionals who contributed their expertise to the construction of the case studies. Our heartfelt thanks goes to Rhonda Goodale, Amanda Welch, and Liz Willner for their invaluable contributions to this text.

A very special acknowledgment also goes to our editor, Laura, who first approached us about this book. She has been our enthusiastic cheerleader through the entire process, offering insightful directions and keeping us motivated. You are amazing!

If twenty million people were infected by a virus that caused anxiety, impulsivity, aggression, sleep problems, depression, respiratory and heart problems, vulnerability to substance abuse, antisocial and criminal behavior, retardation, and school failure, we would consider it an urgent public health crisis. Yet, in the United States alone, there are more than twenty million abused, neglected, and traumatized children vulnerable to these problems. Our society has yet to recognize this epidemic, let alone develop an immunization strategy.

—B. D. Perry

Table of Contents

Introduction 9
How to Use This Book 10

What Is Neglect? 13
Types of Neglect 14
Risk Factors 19
Quiz Me! 22

Fatal Neglect 23
How Are Maltreatment Deaths Identified? 23
Risk Factors for Fatal Neglect 24
Types of Fatal Neglect 26
Quiz Me! 32

Establishing Suspicion 33
Red Flags 33
Assessing Levels of Neglect 36
The Role of Culture, Values, and Community Standards 39
Values and Child Neglect Self-Assessment 40
Handling Disclosure 42
Quiz Me! 43

Making the Report..45
Teacher Fears 46
What You Need 47
Whose Job Is It? 50
Quiz Me! 51

Beyond Reporting: Prevention and Intervention 53
Prevention and Intervention Strategies to Provide to Parents 53
Prevention and Intervention Strategies for Teachers 57
Prevention and Intervention Strategies in the Classroom 60
My Report Card for Neglect Prevention and Intervention 66
Quiz Me! 67

Advocating for Children 69

Conclusion 73

Resources 75
Appendix A. Child Care Self-Assessment:
  Prevention Efforts 79
Appendix B. Ask the Experts: Case Studies for Review
  and Discussion 81
Appendix C. Sample Reporting Form: Making the Call 97
Appendix D. Parent Pages 99
  Early Development and the Brain 100
  Child Abuse Prevention: Learning about Neglect 101
  Motor Vehicle Safety 102
  Fire Safety 103
  Safe Sleeping 104
  Toy Safety 105
  Choosing a Caregiver 106
  Dogs and Children 107
  Accidental Poisoning 108
  Water Safety 109
  Talking with and Listening to Your Child 110
  Playing It Safe at the Park 111
Appendix E. Neglect Issues for the Center or
  School Handbook 113
Appendix F. Child Abuse Hotlines 115
Appendix G: Child Maltreatment Resources 119

The Neglected Child: How to Recognize, Respond, and Prevent was born out of a presentation on child neglect at the National Association for the Education of Young Children (NAEYC) Annual Conference & Expo, which itself emerged out of a need to collect the relatively limited amount of information on child neglect and assemble it into an applied package useful to early childhood professionals, administrators, and students. As this book developed, we could scarcely help but notice that the nightly news seemed to underscore the need for information on child neglect. As we wrote, we heard about the starvation death of a three-month-old baby, born weighing 6 pounds only to die at 3 pounds. Her parents admitted to sometimes forgetting to feed her. We remembered the newborn who was mauled to death by the family puppy as his mother slept in the next room. We worked harder as we heard of the child left in a car at a casino so his father could gamble, the four-year-old who had to go begging neighbors for food because she had been left home alone, and the mother who, without intervening, allowed her boyfriend to beat her child to death. We questioned whether we could write enough to matter for the six-month-old infant who was suffocated by his father in a drug-induced sleep, the toddler whose parents beat him and then denied him lifesaving medical care, and the children who were killed in a fire while locked away in a room. We grieved for these children, and then we wrote more.

The reason we found ourselves so motivated by these cases and the many like them was that, while these children were not killed on purpose, they were not victims of accidents, either. Although each death was tragic and heartrending, none had to happen. These children died because they needed an adult to take care of them, and the person who was supposed to do that did not. A baby must be offered food and a safe place to sleep. A parent must do his or her best to have a safe babysitter for an infant. A toddler who has severe injuries must be taken to a doctor. When a person, whether a parent, a grandparent, or a paid provider, is responsible for taking care of a child and does not do what he or she should to keep the child safe and healthy, that is neglect. These are the types of neglect that result in behavior problems, learning problems, poor growth, and even death. This is the neglect of which we write.

How to Use This Book

Our goal for this book is to make as many caregivers as possible aware of just how pervasive neglect is, how deadly it can be, and perhaps most importantly, that it can be prevented. No child should ever have to suffer neglect if there are adults to intervene. We believe that early childhood professionals are perfectly positioned to identify, intervene in, and prevent neglectful situations, and we have endeavored to give teachers the tools they need to allow more children to grow up safe, happy, and loved. When it comes to neglect, teachers literally can be lifesavers. Test your knowledge by completing the self-assessment in Appendix A (page 79) both before and after reading this book.

A secondary goal for this book is to ensure that no child experiences neglect in an early childhood classroom. Sadly, there are more than a few stories of children who have been neglected and even killed by the people put in place to protect them: child care providers, teachers, and foster parents. As you read this book, think not only of preventing neglect in the home but also of how caregivers can provide a safe, nurturing, and protected environment for the children in their care. The relationships children have with the people who care for them will nourish their brains, bodies, and spirits and can contribute to their healthy and productive development.

The first section of this book provides information about neglect, including different types and levels of severity, establishing suspicion, reporting, and intervening. Each chapter includes a brief quiz that can be used to assess chapter learning or as staff development or continuing education. As you read, you will also see text boxes called "Notes from the Field." These stories, disguised for confidentiality, represent real-life stories that we encountered during the creation of this book. We hope these will inspire discussion and a creative way to apply the material in the chapters.

The second half of this book contains applied materials for teachers/care providers to use for professional development, in staff training, and for parent education. Reproducible and customizable, these include parent handouts on child neglect; sample statements for a parent handbook; self-assessments for teachers, care providers, and directors; and contact numbers for each state and Puerto Rico for reporting suspected neglect. We hope this will prove to be a useful tool kit as you become aware of neglect, and that this information will enable you to create the safest possible classroom environments for the children in your care and to support families to do the same at home.

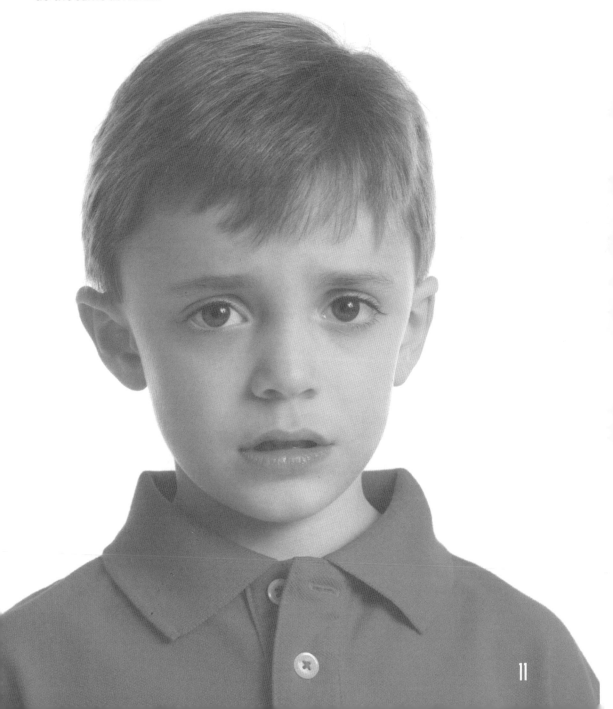

When someone says *child neglect,* what image springs to mind? A hungry child? A child without a winter coat or decent shoes? Families served at soup kitchens, children with matted hair, or those who are unbathed? Do you think poverty and neglect are one and the same? While these images may indeed represent some neglected children, neglect itself is a varied and misunderstood form of child maltreatment.

Many people, even professionals, may see neglected children as the less fortunate or simply "the poor," but not of the same caliber as children who are physically or sexually abused. Images of the "poor but proud" family that suffers with dignity are found everywhere from "The Little Match Girl" of children's literature to *The Grapes of Wrath,* in which John Steinbeck depicts the struggle to survive in noble and heartrending ways. These images are incredibly powerful, yet they show only one face of child neglect.

One of the reasons there can be confusion about neglect is that, unlike sexual abuse or withholding of medical treatment, the federal definition of child neglect is extremely broad and leaves much detail up to the states. There is no overarching federal guideline for the age at which children may be left alone, and no dictum that caregivers must hold babies while they feed them; nor is there any golden rule for how dirty a child must be (or why) to be considered neglected. The details have been left to state governments and to the researchers who study child neglect. The Child Abuse Prevention and Treatment Act (CAPTA) was amended in 2003 to include the definition of child abuse and neglect as, "at a minimum, any recent act or failure to act on the part of a parent or caretaker which results in death, serious physical or emotional harm, sexual abuse or exploitation, or an act or failure to act which presents an imminent risk of serious harm." The CAPTA Reauthorization Act of 2010 provided the foundation on which state definitions are based by establishing a minimum set of standards that define child maltreatment. Each state is then responsible for its own definitions of child abuse and neglect that meet these standards within its civil and criminal codes. The more specific definitions of neglect, as well as the definition of physical abuse, are left up to each state.

A second widely accepted definition of child neglect, which does not specify a degree of harm to the child, is cited by the U.S. Department of Health and Human Services:
"A condition in which a caretaker responsible for the child, either deliberately or by extraordinary inattentiveness, permits the child to experience avoidable present suffering and/or fails to provide one or more of the ingredients generally deemed essential for developing a person's physical, intellectual, and emotional capacities" (Polansky, Hally, & Polansky, 1975).

This second definition adds a new element to assessing neglect in that the behavior creates or contributes to a lack of something "deemed essential" for the child's development and well-being. Essential elements can be defined both culturally and regionally and can vary from state to state. It is important for teachers to understand the basics of child development, health, and safety, as well as local standards for child care. This means that your personal beliefs, feelings, history, and values, and even where you live, can shape what you see as neglect.

Types of Neglect

Even among researchers who study child abuse and neglect, more study abuse. Some have even commented that the study of neglect is itself a neglected area (Dubowitz, 2007). The relatively few people who have studied neglect have created a number of categories by which neglect can be identified. We have consolidated those categories for you here, but be aware that if you read much about neglect, you will see these categories called by several different names. The concepts, we believe, remain very similar. In addition to these discrete categories, there are degrees of neglectful behavior, such as *chronic* (occurring as part of a pattern) or *acute* (occurs just one time).

When all of the components of child neglect are examined, we can discern six different kinds of neglect that affect children and their families. (See Table 2.1, page 21.) The type in which children lack clothing, food, or shelter is generally termed *physical neglect* or *deprivation of needs neglect*. This means that children's basic physical needs are not being met. This type of neglect is generally chronic, meaning that it occurs in a persistent pattern in which a child is not cared for appropriately. We all know that young children are prone to refuse a meal or throw a tantrum over wearing a coat; however, it is not the isolated skipped meal that creates neglect. It is a pattern of a child being denied adequate nutrition that defines this type of neglect. Deprivation, like all forms of neglect, is perpetrated by a person responsible for the child, sometimes called the PRC. Parents are responsible but so are child caregivers, babysitters, and other adults left to care for a child. If you are in charge of providing a child with a safe and healthy environment, you can neglect a child in the failure to do so.

Another type of neglect is *medical neglect*. In this type of neglect, children are denied needed medical care to treat a condition or prevent the worsening of a condition or a life-threatening event or illness. This type of neglect may be either chronic, as when a child is repeatedly refused medical care for an ongoing condition, or acute. It also may take the form of a family member or caregiver failing to heed obvious signs of illness or trauma. Acute medical neglect means that a child is in need of but is denied one-time or emergency medical care. The American Academy of Pediatrics previously has published an opinion rejecting such parental rights (American Academy of Pediatrics, 1997). The prevention of medical neglect through the withholding of life-sustaining medical care was reaffirmed in the 2010 CAPTA reauthorization. Caregivers need to be aware that their responsibility is to always protect the child by making a report of medical neglect or by alerting medical personnel in an emergency situation. No caregiver should ever fail to make a report based on either his or her own or the family's religious beliefs.

A third type of neglect is *supervisory neglect*. Supervisory neglect occurs when a person responsible for a child (the PRC) either fails to supervise that child to keep him or her from harm or fails to have someone responsible and able to care for the child do so. Examples of this type of neglect include a parent who sends a toddler outside to play and fails to watch the child to keep him or her safe, a parent who leaves a child in the care of someone who is using or passed out from drugs or alcohol, or a home child care provider who leaves a child alone near a water source in which he or she could fall or drown. This type of neglect, too, can be chronic and acute. Chronic supervisory neglect might entail a parent who routinely leaves a toddler alone in a house while he or she goes to work. An example of an acute supervision problem might be a parent who, on only one occasion, fails to put away a loaded gun and leaves it where a child might access it.

15

Environmental neglect is a fourth type, although it may appear to be related to both deprivation of needs and supervisory neglect. Children who suffer environmental neglect may come from filthy homes. This can include circumstances such as dirty dishes, rotting food left out, or infestations of rats or cockroaches. Children who come from such environments may come to school regularly in unwashed clothing or without having been bathed recently. This is why some professionals group environmental and needs neglect together.

"We Should Have Sued"

When my son was 18 months old, he attended a home day care center. One day, my husband went to pick him up, and the provider couldn't find him. The house was searched frantically, and the police were called. Fortunately, our 911 call was connected to a lost child who had been found two hours earlier wandering in a busy intersection. He had been taken home by a stranger who, thankfully, called the police. The provider had no idea my child had wandered out her unlocked front door until pickup time. He could have been killed or kidnapped, or met with any number of horrible things. To this day, I don't know why I didn't sue the provider for everything she was worth. I suppose I was just so glad that my child was alive I didn't care about her.

Educational neglect, by definition, may be difficult to assess because not only may children neglected in this manner miss school, but their parents may have failed to register them at all. For school-age children who are required to attend school, parents may create a neglectful environment by avoiding the school because they do not like it, because they can not find the electric bill or birth certificate to register the child, or to prevent a child from reporting abuse or other family secrets. Parents also may be unable or uninterested in engaging in efforts to enroll their child in, help their child get ready for, or transport their child to school. For infants and preschool children who have been registered for group care, teachers may notice a pattern of absences that may be due to parents keeping children at home to let abuse injuries heal. Children also are sometimes kept from school to care for younger children in the absence of a parent, or perhaps even to care for an incapacitated parent. However, there are many reasons that a parent may hide a child from the educational system at any age.

The final category we use to describe neglect is *emotional neglect*. Some researchers do not use this classification by itself because they think it fits better with other categories. However, we feel strongly that it is a unique form of neglect. Emotional neglect is like deprivation of needs neglect except, instead of physical needs, it is the child's emotional needs that go unmet or inappropriately met. For instance, child care professionals acknowledge that the most important goal of the first year of life is to establish the attachment relationship between the infant and his or her caregivers. Unpredictable parents who love one minute and punish the next, parents who regularly ignore children's needs and cries, and families that are chaotic or violent can all disrupt the development of secure attachment. Although there are many reasons for a parent to not meet a child's emotional needs, such as maternal depression, drug or alcohol abuse, or simply not knowing how to react to a baby, all of these behaviors can be classified as neglectful, regardless of the root cause. The consequences of emotional neglect are serious and far-reaching, including nonorganic failure to thrive (which can lead to a child's death), social problems with same-age peers, attention problems, aggression, and an impaired ability to form satisfying relationships.

Remember, if it SEEMED like neglect, report it!

Admittedly, remembering these six categories of neglect can be confusing. A simple mnemonic is, "If it SEEMED like neglect, report it." Each letter in SEEMED represents one area of neglect, listed below with some examples.

S: Supervisory neglect
- Failing to supervise a young child around water, weapons, or other dangerous circumstances
- Supervising a child while impaired on illegal or prescription drugs or alcohol
- Leaving a child with an impaired caregiver
- Leaving unsupervised a child who cannot be expected to handle a crisis adequately

E: Environmental neglect

- Rotten food, cockroaches, or vermin in the home
- Feces on the floor
- Piles of soiled diapers or clothing
- Children covered in insect or rodent bites
- Infants with feces, blood, or rotten food stuck to them
- Children with cockroaches in their diapers
- Children kept in a home with dangerous and available weapons or drugs

E: Educational neglect

- Not taking a school-age child to school for any reason
- Not taking a child to school to hide abuse or illicit family activities
- Not taking a child to school because of a lack of resources or proof of residence

M: Medical neglect

- Withholding care from an injured infant with the intent to cause death
- Failing to secure care for a child's chronic condition
- Failing to secure medical attention for an injured child

E: Emotional neglect

- Humiliating a child
- Engaging in bizarre forms of punishment
- Rejecting a child
- Blaming a child for the family's problems (scapegoating)

D: Deprivation of needs neglect

- Withholding food or water
- Abandoning a baby or child to the elements
- Failing to protect a baby from the elements (because of inadequate shelter or clothing, as opposed to abandonment)

Risk Factors

For all of the above forms of child neglect, there are certain environmental conditions that researchers have associated with nonfatal neglect. (For a discussion on the unique risks for fatal neglect, please see that chapter). Barth (2009) found that substance abuse, mental illness, domestic violence, and child conduct problems alone or in combination are associated with child maltreatment. Stagner and Lansing (2009) also included small, sparse social networks, community disorganization, and violence as risk factors. Risk factors such as poverty, isolation, and depression rarely happen independently, and each factor can magnify the effects of other factors. Substance abuse, lower economic status, depression and other mental health conditions, a history of neglect, membership in a cultural minority, and rural or urban locations may indicate higher risk of abuse and neglect; however, child neglect can occur in any family or any classroom without regard to family income level or circumstance.

Substance abuse: Drug use can lead caregivers to place a higher priority on obtaining the drug than on providing for children's needs for food, clothing, hygiene, and medical care. Failing to provide basic needs is the most common type of neglect associated with substance abuse (Barth, 2009). When parents are addicted to drugs or alcohol, they are not intellectually available to practice good parenting. Emotional maturity may be stunted by drug use, leading to poor choices.

Economic factors: The relationship between poverty and neglect is complex; while poverty is associated with certain kinds of neglect (deprivation of needs), it is not associated with other kinds (fatalities or emotional neglect). Additionally, the definitions of poverty and certain types of neglect share the overlapping characteristics of deprivation of clothing, shelter, food, and/or care (Child Information Gateway, 2007). Thus, it can be difficult to fully distinguish the two concepts. When caregivers suspect neglect, however, a report must be made to child protection regardless of the reason why neglect may be occurring. To clarify, the determination of whether a child lacks necessary care or resources due to neglect, poverty, or a combination of the two is made after a report is initiated with child protection.

Mental health factors: One of the most frequently examined mental health factors is maternal depression. Maternal depression has been linked to emotional and behavioral problems in children, which can lead to further difficulties in parenting; likewise, studies have found that when a mother's depression and stress decreased, her nurturing increased. Other parental mental health conditions, when untreated, also can contribute to chaotic or unpredictable parenting styles, to difficulties getting children to school, and to potential decreases in a parent's ability to hold a steady job and provide basic needs. Parents' stress levels can be decreased by having someone to talk to and feeling that they have someone who understands what they are going through. Their children's caregivers can provide these things just by listening, reserving judgment, and providing social opportunities for parents to connect with each other.

Maternal Depression

According to the American Academy of Pediatrics (2010) 400,000 infants are born to depressed mothers each year; additionally, the American Psychological Association (2012) estimates that 9 percent–16 percent of all postpartum women will experience postpartum depression. Younger women, those who receive Medicaid, and those with lower levels of formal education have been found to have increased incidences of postpartum depression when compared to their peers. (Brett, Barfield, & Williams, 2008)

Family history: Some researchers have explored an intergenerational cycle of neglect in which parents repeat the adverse experiences that they experienced as children (Wilson & Mullin, 2010). Parents may choose to parent as they were parented or may simply revert to a pattern of what they remember when other techniques do not seem to work as they expected.

Social groups: Children from ethnic minority groups are overrepresented in the child protection system when compared to base rates in the population; however, it is unclear if differences are due to income level, reporting and system bias, or true cultural differences (Self-Brown et al., 2011).

Geographic location: Family isolation can occur in both rural and urban settings. A lack of connection to friends, family, and the community means a lack of support networks in stressful times. Families may intentionally isolate themselves due to social anxiety, but often the demands of raising children, especially for single parents, can leave little time or energy for meeting people or maintaining social relationships, causing unintentional separation from support systems. The more people a child interacts with, the greater the chance someone will be aware of mistreatment.

Table 2.1 Summary of Neglect Types

Type of Neglect	May Be Chronic	May Be Acute	Potentially Fatal
Deprivation of Needs	X		
Medical	X	X	Yes
Supervisory	X	X	Yes
Educational	X	X	Potentially (Absences can be used as a cover for abuse.)
Emotional	X		Yes (Failure to thrive)
Environmental	X	X	Yes

Quiz Me!

This quiz can be used as a self-assessment for this chapter.

1. A parent often has no food in the house and, because of her work schedule, has to leave her six-year-old son home alone with her four-year-old and two-year-old. What types of neglect should you suspect?
   a. educational and supervisory
   b. emotional and deprivation of needs
   c. deprivation of needs and supervisory
   d. medical and supervisory

2. Who is considered to be a person responsible for a child (PRC)?
   a. a parent
   b. a child care provider
   c. a babysitter
   d. all of the above

3. Which type of neglect is characterized by a filthy or rodent-infested home, a chronically dirty child, or a home filled with rotting food?
   a. deprivation of needs
   b. environmental neglect
   c. medical neglect
   d. supervisory neglect

4. A child who is unpredictably shuffled between homes, often left with caregivers he or she does not know, and often supervised overnight by individuals who are incapacitated by drugs may be experiencing what types of neglect? (Choose all that apply.)
   a. medical
   b. emotional
   c. environmental
   d. supervisory
   e. deprivation of needs
   f. educational

5. Fill in the blank: Some risk factors for emotional neglect include parental substance abuse, a lack of knowledge about child development, and _____, which can cause parents to be unresponsive to infants' needs.

Answers: c; d; b; b and d; depression

One of the reasons that child neglect may receive less attention than other forms of child maltreatment, both in research and in the public eye, is that it is often considered to occur less often and be less serious than other types of abuse. However, this is a very big misrepresentation of child neglect. In 2010, an estimated 695,000 children were identified as being abused and/or neglected in the United States, which equates to just more than nine children out of every 1,000 (U.S. Department of Health and Human Services, 2010). Of these cases, an overwhelming 78.3 percent were the result of neglect. Although child physical and sexual abuse are often the types of maltreatment most commonly perceived by the general public, child neglect alone constitutes nearly one third of all child maltreatment fatalities. When present, neglect has been found to be accompanied by abuse in 95 percent of cases (Mennen, Kim, Sang, & Trickett, 2010).

A child's life lost is the ultimate price for neglectful adult behavior. And yet, neglect is considered by many to be nonfatal or even not worth reporting. With 1,500 children estimated to die each year from child maltreatment in the United States and more than 33 percent of those attributed to neglect alone, a substantial number of young children die due to nothing other than negligence each year. This number does not include children who die from abuse or those whose deaths are ruled to be due to combined abuse and neglect.

How Are Maltreatment Deaths Identified?

All states and the District of Columbia have a Child Death Review Board. You can find yours here: www.childdeathreview.org. These boards are charged with creating a team of professionals from a variety of specialties to review all child deaths, with the idea that we must understand child deaths before we can prevent them. Much of what we know about the ways in which children die has come from these boards.

The boards, which review individually the deaths of all children, use data from death certificates, state child protective services, hospital records, police records, and cause-of-death determinations by medical examiners to explore the preventable ways in which children die. This approach, by which many sources of information are obtained, is considered the best. States that use only one source, such as medical-examiner rulings, are thought to underestimate the incidences of child death from maltreatment. This may explain some state-to-state variation in fatality data.

Risk Factors for Fatal Neglect

Much of the research about child maltreatment fatalities combines neglect with abuse; however, because neglect and abuse often co-occur, it is critical for caregivers to understand these risk factors. When we talk about risk factors, we mean characteristics of a child, family, or home that have been more associated with children who die from maltreatment than with children who do not die. These risk factors are said to be correlated with child maltreatment fatalities; they do not necessarily cause the child's death, but they are associated with deaths. Some of the risk factors for child fatalities include the child's age and household composition. (See Table 3.1, page 30.)

First, the younger a child is, the higher the risk for maltreatment fatality. Children younger than the age of one year are at particular risk, and this risk is elevated throughout the first few years of life. According to one study, 65 percent of fatal child neglect occurred for children under the age of one year (Klevens & Leeb, 2010). Infants in their first year may be particularly vulnerable to fatal child abuse and neglect because, when they are maltreated, they can not fight back, are unable to clearly communicate that they are being abused, and may be less likely to be seen by others outside of a small circle of caregivers. They are also the most vulnerable to even brief physical insults.

Children younger than five years old have been found to have an increased risk for fatal abuse and neglect if they are living in a house with one or more adults who are not related to them, such as their mother's boyfriend, and if they are living with step-, foster, or adoptive parents. Young children who reside with just one parent but no other unrelated adults have not been found to be at increased risk for fatal maltreatment (Stiffman, Schnitzer, Adam, Kruse, & Ewigman, 2002). This is particularly interesting because it is not the mere number of adults available to supervise and protect a child that matters; it is the relationship between the child and the caregiver that makes a child vulnerable to maltreatment fatalities. Caregivers need to be particularly aware of the substantial risks for fatal neglect that exist for infants in all circumstances and for young children who reside in homes with unrelated adults. Some of those specific fatality risks are detailed below.

Failure to supervise children appropriately is the most common cause of fatal neglect.

Finally, the failure of adults to properly supervise young children has been found, overall, to be the leading factor in both child neglect and child neglect deaths (Bonner, Crow, & Logue, 1999). Deaths due to accidents or "unintentional injury" are carefully investigated as some are due to negligence, as in the case of improper supervision, while others are ruled accidental death not due to negligence on the part of a person responsible for the child. This is often a fine line, and states do not always agree about what is an accident and what is negligence. This is further complicated by the fact, as we discussed in the chapter "What Is Neglect?", that negligent supervision can occur in one instance or over time as a pattern. An example of unintentional injury or death may be a sober parent who forgets that a sleeping young child is in the car and leaves the child there as he or she goes off to work. There is no intent to leave the child in the car, nor was the parent mindful of the child and merely negligent in the child's care. The error was due to memory or distraction problems. The same case may be viewed as negligence if a parent chooses to leave the child in the car all day or forgets and leaves the child there because the adult is impaired with drugs or alcohol. While the caregiver's intent is not always considered an important factor in assessing neglect, it is a more important consideration when assessing fatal neglect.

Types of Fatal Neglect

Smothering and Asphyxiation

Infants can be smothered because an adult sleeps with them (sometimes called co-sleeping); because they are left with an older sibling or other inappropriate caregiver who accidentally rolls over on them or knocks a pillow onto them; because they are put into a crib with blankets, bumpers, pillows, or stuffed animals, which block their airways; or because they are left alone in an unsafe environment such as near a plastic bag. Infants can also die from choking on small objects or from a cord, a rope, or another item wrapping around their necks. Infants who sleep in an adult bed are 20 times more likely to die than infants who sleep alone in a safe crib. And infants are not the only ones at risk for suffocation. In the year 2000 alone, 842 children died from accidental suffocation in the United States (www.childdeathreview.org). However, more recent data from Safe Kids USA indicated that nearly 1,100 children aged 14 years and under died from accidental suffocation in 2009.

Falls and Head Injuries

Both infants who are mobile, such as crawlers, and those who cannot yet crawl but may be able to roll are at risk for falls due to neglect. Serious head trauma, such as a traumatic brain injury (TBI), or even death can result. Infants who are not appropriately supervised can easily fall from a bed, a changing table, or another location where they are left unattended. Infants who are becoming mobile can begin to pull up on objects and are at risk for being crushed by toppling items. Several infants and toddlers have pulled large television sets onto themselves and have tragically died as a result.

Pets

Children younger than the age of one year can be killed by being left inappropriately supervised near pets. Pets as seemingly harmless as small puppies have fatally assaulted infants left helpless without supervision. Animals are not able to reliably resist biting and chewing; an infant left on a floor or strapped into a swing or seat is a helpless victim.

Drowning

Drowning has been identified as the leading cause of child neglect fatalities. Children younger than age one are at risk for this type of fatality when they are left unsupervised or inappropriately supervised. This may occur when children are purposefully playing in water such as a swimming pool or a bathtub, or when they are unintentionally left with poor or no supervision and come into contact with water. These types of drowning include children who fall into buckets, outdoor fountains, toilets, or other sources. Finally, environmental neglect may be present when children are not provided with a safe way to interact with water. An example of this may include a young child who falls from a boat while being supervised yet does not have on a life jacket recommended for his or her age.

Deprivation of Needs

Because infants younger than age one year are totally dependent on their adult caregivers, they are at particular risk for death from dehydration and malnutrition. When infants' physical needs are neglected, they may quickly die. They are also very susceptible to issues related to abandonment, which may include not being given food or water as well as not being provided physical shelter. A related fatal neglect concept is that of failure to thrive (FTT). FTT is diagnosed by a medical doctor and can be indicated by an infant who fails to grow as expected. Some FTT is due to metabolic conditions such as Crohn's disease, while other FTT is due to neglect. FTT is an interesting concept in fatal neglect in that it can occur both in infants who are not being fed appropriately, such as those who are not given enough food, and in those who are given inappropriate food (e.g., infants who are expected to eat pizza or steak instead of baby formula or breast milk), as well as those who are fed but not nurtured. Babies who are not held and talked to while being fed can exhibit delayed growth. Babies require nurturance to use the nutrition they are given. This type of neglect is also related to emotional neglect.

Both infants and older children are susceptible to starvation, dehydration, and abandonment, all of which are characteristics of fatal deprivation of needs neglect.

Fires

Improper fire safety can be fatal for a child of any age. Young infants are obviously at risk because they can neither understand the warning signs of a fire nor get themselves to safety. They are at risk for death due to fire because of environmental neglect (not having working smoke detectors) as well as lack of supervision (being left at home alone or with an incapacitated or other inappropriate caregiver). These risks remain throughout early childhood, although the risk for death due to inadequate supervision also includes children who accidentally start fires while not being supervised.

A note about supervision: A theme throughout these early chapters has been children who are left without a caregiver, with a caregiver who is incapacitated by drugs or alcohol, or with a caregiver who is unable to care for them such as someone who is too young or physically unable. When you are assessing whether or not a supervision arrangement is suspect for neglect, you must consider not only whether or not a child can be fine if left at home alone but also whether or not a child will be fine if left alone and an emergency happens. Young children easily can become confused or frightened if an emergency, such as a smoke detector going off in a fire or storm sirens sounding, occurs. Children may perish while hiding as a fire rages or may injure a younger sibling in their care while trying to save him or her from perceived danger. A supervision arrangement must be adequate in a dangerous situation as well as in a situation in which nothing goes wrong.

Notes from the Field

Trying to Do Their Best

Four children were killed in a house fire when the shed they were sleeping in caught fire. Their parents were having a party in the main house and put their two children, as well as a niece and nephew, to bed in an outbuilding so they wouldn't be exposed to the drinking and drugs that were planned for the party. Because the neighborhood did have registered sex offenders, the parents placed a strong padlock on the outside of the shed, gave the children snacks and water, and plugged in a space heater. They intended to bring the children back into the house after they had sobered up from the party the next morning. The space heater caught fire, however, near the end of the party, and the children were unable to escape or be rescued.

Medical Neglect

Medical neglect can occur for a child of any age and can be fatal at any age. It is neglectful for a caregiver to fail to obtain medical care in a timely manner to prevent a condition from becoming serious or lifethreatening, and it is neglectful for a caregiver to deny a child medical care that can reasonably be expected to correct a life-threatening condition. Under no circumstances is it legally acceptable for a caregiver, including medical personnel, to withhold food or water from an infant, no matter how ill or irreversible the medical condition. This law is sometimes called the Baby Doe Law or Baby Doe Amendment. It mandates that any state receiving federal funds for child abuse and neglect programs must have in place procedures to report medical neglect. In essence, this law prohibits individuals or institutions from withholding lifesaving care from disabled newborns. It is not legal to facilitate a newborn's death because the infant was born with a disability.

Examples of medical neglect that can lead to a fatality include a child who receives a head injury but is denied treatment, a child who is denied lifesaving surgery, or a child from whom necessary medication is withheld. We also consider psychiatric neglect to fall under this category, which would include a failure to secure psychiatric help for a child who is acutely suicidal. Other classification systems may list this as emotional neglect; nevertheless, the withholding of potentially lifesaving intervention, be it physical or psychological, can be fatal.

Motor Vehicle Collisions

We use the term *motor vehicle collision* (MVC) in this book instead of the more generic term *accident* for two reasons. First, neglect occurs because a person responsible for the child fails to meet appropriate child protection guidelines. Second, in regard to child neglect, there are no "accidents"; events occur for human-caused reasons.

Children, particularly those who are unrestrained, are extremely susceptible to traumatic brain injuries and death stemming from MVCs. The installation and proper use of child safety seats is key and is a primary area of prevention for child care providers. Other driving practices that may be considered neglectful are the transportation of a child while the driver is intoxicated on alcohol or other substances that impair abilities, and the deliberate use of a motor vehicle in such a manner that endangers a child passenger. This may include a parent who crashes a car purposefully in an effort to injure another person, one who charges a police car in a chase, or one who deliberately crashes into another car in a fit of road rage.

Poisoning

Young children are naturally curious and prone to explore any unguarded purse, drawer, cabinet, or bottle. This puts them at risk for finding and ingesting any unguarded amount of alcohol; prescription, nonprescription, or illicit drugs; household cleansers; or even toxic cosmetic products. While many poisoning incidents and even deaths are ruled accidental, poisonings can be classified as neglect if they are due to a lack of appropriate supervision (i.e., no caregiver or an inappropriate or intoxicated caregiver) and more rarely can be connected to other forms of maltreatment such as abuse. Poisoning as a form of abuse may include instances of forcing a child to ingest alcohol or poison for any reason.

Table 3.1 Key Developmental Stages and Causes of Death

Age	Developmental characteristics	Fatal neglect deaths

Infants (< 1 year)	Complete dependence on caregivers for:
	  - adequate nutrition
	  - sensory stimulation
	  - emotional support
	Rapid physical growth
	Postural ability develops
	  - head control
	  - roll over
	  - sit alone (seven months)
	Limited strength
	Ability to crawl (ten months)
	Limited social sphere
		Drowning
		Suffocation
		Overheating
		Malnutrition
		Dehydration
		Treatable diseases and
		  conditions (e.g., pneumonia)

Toddlers (1–4 years)	Rapid growth and motor
	  development (fine and gross)
	Mobility: walk, climb
	High levels of physical activity
	Curious and exploratory
		Drowning
		Motor transport fatalities:
		  pedestrians, passengers
		Fires

Toddlers (1–4 years)	Limited balance and coordination Cannot stop/turn suddenly Egocentric thinking No/limited awareness of hazards No/limited concept of rules Copy others Overestimate their ability	Scalding Malnutrition Treatable diseases
Middle Childhood–Adolescence (5–12 years)	Gross motor skills developing and mastered Increased strength Difficulty judging speed/distance Learning through play and get caught up in play Aware of common hazards Reaction time slow Increasing importance of peer relationships Expanding social sphere	Motor transport fatalities: pedestrians, passengers Drownings Fires
Teenagers (13–17 years)	Increased social mobility Independence Sense of invulnerability Experimentation and risk taking	Risk taking (e.g., transport fatalities, falls, alcohol-related fatalities) Drug overdoses Suicide Eating disorders (e.g., anorexia)

Reprinted with permission from Lawrence, R., & Irvine, P. (2004). "Redefining fatal child neglect." *Child Abuse Prevention Issues, 21* Accessed June 11, 2011. *http://www.aifs.gov.au/nch/pubs/issues/ issues21/issues21.html*

It is very important to understand that no child of any age is immune from fatal neglect; however, the younger a child is, the greater the risk that even one instance of neglect can become fatal. This means that there is perhaps a special burden for infant and toddler caregivers. Any suspicion of neglect needs to be reported; all caregivers must be aware that neglect has the potential to take a child's life.

Quiz Me!

1. A child who sleeps in bed with an adult has a risk of death _____ times greater than that of a child who sleeps alone in a crib.
   a. 5
   b. 10
   c. 15
   d. 20

2. Which of the following are risk factors for a child maltreatment fatality (choose all that apply)?
   a. living with a single mother
   b. being younger than the age of 1 year
   c. living with adults who are nonrelations
   d. living in a low-income intact family

3. Which of the following is the leading cause of death due to child neglect?
   a. drowning
   b. poisoning
   c. medical neglect
   d. fire

4. Which agency, present in every state, is responsible for reviewing all child deaths?
   a. Child Protective Services
   b. Office of the medical examiner
   c. Local and state police
   d. Child Death Review Board

5. Approximately how many children are confirmed to be abused or neglected in a year in the United States?
   a. nearly 700,000
   b. nearly 10,000
   c. nearly 1,500
   d. nearly 9,000

6. Which type of child maltreatment accounts for the largest percentage of child maltreatment reports in the United States?
   a. physical abuse
   b. neglect
   c. sexual abuse
   d. none of the above

Answers: d; b and c; a; d; a; b

Because neglect is a serious and even fatal form of child maltreatment, it is certainly reportable to child protection authorities. However, many teachers feel confused about the standard of suspicion. What does it mean to be suspicious? What if your suspicion is not the same as another teacher's suspicion? To help you translate your feelings into reportable suspicion, we will cover the following guidelines:

- Understand what *suspicion* means
- Understand the types, levels, and risk factors for neglect
- Connect your values to suspicion

As trained caregivers, we share a special burden to be aware of the signs of neglect. Caregivers are expected to know more about how and when to suspect neglect than a layperson. In fact, one of the standards for reporting suspicion is whether you "should" have suspected and reported neglect. For example, if you failed to report neglect that resulted in a child's death, you might be confronted in court with examples of other teachers with your level of training and experience who agree that you should have known to report.

Red Flags

Red flag is a term used to indicate warning. For teachers, it can mean that environmental or behavioral issues are signaling that it is time to get some help. This can mean peer consultation, making an official report, or both. Teachers can ask advice from administrators, counselors, child development specialists, or other professionals in the school or community, but ultimately no advice will relieve a teacher of his or her duty to report. No other person can give permission to report or not report; teachers must use their professional judgment to act in the best interest of a child based on the information available at the time. It is our job as teachers to suspect and the work of child protective services to decide. However, there are some tools that we can use to help translate our uneasy feelings into reportable suspicion.

Should have known is an important standard, because it means that you are expected to understand child neglect and report it. It does not matter if you did not receive good training, if you were sick the day of a training, or if the training was not offered. You must know the material. Annual training in child maltreatment is vital for all child caregivers, but we also offer a list of some red flags of child neglect.

Symptoms that may catch teachers' attention include the behavioral and the physical. Children may have frequent school absences, steal or hoard food, use drugs or alcohol, experience developmental delays, or display bizarre and inappropriate behavior. Children who are overly parental or adultlike, as well as those who act developmentally inappropriately as though they are babies, can also raise red flags. Children who are either overly compliant or overly defiant also can be exhibiting problematic behaviors. Children who have been neglected often have had their cravings for and efforts toward warm, loving relationships denied. Perhaps their caregivers have refused their hugs, made fun of them for crying, or crushed an innocently picked "bouquet" of flowers from the yard. If a child has been raised to be always or almost always rejected, he or she may be unable to show love or affection toward others. If you have a child in your classroom who seems unable to seek your approval, attention, or pleasurable interaction, he or she may be a child who has experienced emotional neglect.

Notes from the Field

"It's a Great Babysitter"
One day I was complaining about trying to find a babysitter for my oldest child for the upcoming weekend, when one of my colleagues offered to help out. At first I was so relieved, but then he told me what his plan was: He said that he liked to take his five- and eight-year-old children to a large, local waterpark and drop them off. He seemed very proud that he was able to get a day to get his errands run while his kids had fun. When I asked about how safe that was, he assured me that his kids "knew better" than to do anything unsafe. I didn't wind up using him for child care after all.

Physical signs that teachers may see include children without appropriate clothing, children who regularly present to school dirty and foul smelling, and children who are in obvious need of medical care, including dental or vision. However, be aware that some signs of child neglect also can be observed in the child's caregiver. These may include a parent who is cruel, punishing, or inappropriate to the child in your presence; one who expresses no interest in and/or pays little attention to the child; and one who appears to abuse drugs or alcohol. The use of alcohol is not neglectful; however, when a child fails to receive attention, supervision, affection, or basic care so that a parent can obtain, use, or recover from an addiction, it is a problem. Neglectful parents may also be excessively demanding and out of sync with their child's development, may refuse needed physical or educational services, and may request that you as a teacher engage in bizarre or inappropriate child guidance.

"Something for Him, Something for Me"
Durant arrived at kindergarten a few days after the school year started. He was excited to meet his classmates and me, his teacher. As we started down the hallway, his mother handed him a baby bottle of milk to drink. I looked quizzically at the mother, who said, "I have my coffee; he has his bottle." When Durant entered the classroom, I suggested he put the bottle and his backpack in his cubby. He never asked for it, and the bottle didn't come back to school.

There are also social signs of neglect. Children who are neglected may seem a bit "different" in your classroom, with signs worsening over time. Children who are neglected have been found to have fewer social interactions with classmates and more aggression than children who are not neglected (Hoffman-Plotkin & Twentyman, 1984). Other researchers have found that neglected children handle stress poorly, often seeming helpless when faced with obstacles (Crittenden & Ainsworth, 1989). Because the classroom is filled with new and challenging experiences on a daily basis, neglected children may become overwhelmed and helpless. This can be displayed as passivity, tearfulness, avoidance, or aggression. When children are failing to explore as they should, look for a cause for this behavior. It may be neglect. When assessing for neglect, however, remember that a neglected child also may suffer abuse and that children who are neglected can present differently than children who suffer from both abuse and neglect. The types of educational signs that you may see include learning problems, achievement problems, and developmental delays. A review of 17 years of studies on neglect found that educational problems are more severe for children who are neglected than for children who are abused (Katz, 1992).

When many of these signs are viewed out of context, it is impossible to tell if a behavior is neglectful, abusive, or benign; additionally, some signs are indicative of other diagnoses unrelated to neglect.

For some signs, such as an intoxicated or violent parent, waiting to document the incident would not be in the best interest of the child and his or her safety. However, in other cases where an isolated incident does not present a threat to the child and does not in itself reach the criteria for suspicion, documentation can be helpful. Remember, however, if you are suspicious, you must document the incident *and* call child protective services. Do not merely document if you are already suspicious.

If you do observe a behavior that you think you need to track to establish suspicion, and that behavior does not pose a threat to the child's immediate well-being, it can be a good idea to make a note in your lesson plan or attendance book to help you keep track of important days or times when the behavior is observed. This can help you establish a pattern. Notice if there seems to be a problem first thing in the morning or when the child may be tired, before lunch or snack when the child may be hungry, or at the end of the day when routines may be more relaxed. If you are not sure what to make of something, ask a trusted colleague, school counselor, or administrator. Be careful to respect the confidentiality of families by sharing relevant information while avoiding gossip. Remember that sharing concerns within your school does not replace the requirement to make a report to your state's child protection agency if maltreatment is suspected.

Assessing Levels of Neglect

A child maltreatment expert, Diane DePanfilis (2006), has described three levels of neglect: mild, moderate, and severe. It is critical for teachers to understand these levels as they take action to prevent, intervene, and report a neglectful situation to authorities.

As we discussed before, neglect is assessed as either a chronic condition or an isolated incident. It is also assessed by whether or not the harm or, in some cases, the threat of harm is mild, moderate, or severe. If the harm to a child is none or minimal and the frequency of occurrence is rare, this may be an instance of mild neglect. DePanfilis offers the example of a child who is not restrained in a car seat as an example of mild neglect; however, one also may consider the potential harm to a child, which in this case may be severe (death or maiming injury), when deciding whether or not to report.

Table 4.1 presents a decision-making grid for assessing potential neglect and making a decision to prevent, intervene, or report. Children may have multiple levels of neglect. These are only examples, and teachers should always report suspected neglect to allow the authorities to assess actual risk.

Table 4.1 Levels of Neglect Severity

	Isolated example	Chronic example	Likely level of neglect	Most suitable strategies
No actual harm	Parent accidentally locks toddler in car and immediately calls for backup keys and gets child out.	Parent routinely feeds child junk food for breakfast.	None Mild	Prevention and intervention through parent education
Minimal harm or risk of harm	Parent forgets child's coat one day in winter, and child must wait 10 minutes at bus stop.	Child is dressed inappropriately for winter weather, lacking coat or shoes.	Mild Moderate	Prevention or intervention (organizational strategies; providing backup emergency coats at school) Moderate: intervention (referral to resource agency) and reportable
Risk of injury or actual injury	Parents send a young child across a street one time to buy soda.	Child with diabetes does not receive medication or medical care.	Moderate Severe	Moderate: prevention, intervention, reportable Severe: reportable; after reporting, intervention
Risk of serious injury/death or actual serious injury/death	Intoxicated parent puts child in car and speeds down the highway with the child unrestrained in the back seat.	Caregiver takes young children to a lake and then naps in car while they play unsupervised.	Severe	Reportable; after reporting, intervention and prevention of further problems

No doubt this chart leaves you with as many questions as answers. That is the difficulty when classifying the nuances of neglect. Some experts have argued that the caregivers' intentions should be weighed when assessing neglect; whereas, others convincingly argue that neglect can occur without anyone being "at fault." Indeed, there may be a difference between a parent who forgets a coat (this has happened to nearly all parents), those who cannot afford a coat, and those who punish their child by refusing to allow the child to have a coat. None of the children in these scenarios has a coat. What information do you rely on to decide whether or not to report an incident? Does the "why" matter if a child is in need?

Certainly, you rely on whether the neglect is chronic or acute; a one-time instance without a coat in mild winter weather can be forgiven or accommodated and likely will not require from alerting the authorities. A child whose family cannot afford a coat may benefit from help either from the child protective services system, which would necessitate reporting, or, if no other instances of neglect are suspected, perhaps from school assistance and community services. Finally, for the child who is punished by being subjected to winter weather without protection, this is the most likely scenario in which multiple services from child protection (resources, education) can be beneficial. This would necessitate a report.

To create such a report, caregivers must make a variety of information: chronic or acute condition, parental intent, risk of harm to the child, and actual harm to the child. Nationally, the criterion for reporting is suspicion of child abuse, not proof. As you work to determine whether neglect is present and, if so, what type and degree of neglect, it may be helpful to make a chart for yourself. You may be surprised to discover that your "uneasy feelings" about a child's well-being actually translate to multiple types and levels of neglect.

The criterion for reporting child maltreatment is suspicion, not proof.

The Role of Culture, Values, and Community Standards

When establishing suspicion of neglect, one of the first things most people reference is what is considered neglectful where they live. This is an automatic process in which people apply the community standard for child well-being. Think of where you live. Is it normal to raise a child in a home without electricity or indoor plumbing? to bathe a child only once a week? If you live in the United States, it is probably not the typical way to live. However, just a few generations ago, much of the rural United States lived this way. In a community in which electricity and water in the home are considered a necessity, a child who lives without these utilities may make you question whether the child's basic needs are being met.

Which of the following options are acceptable (i.e., not neglectful) for where you live?

1. A three-year-old child who is:
- fed cold cereal for breakfast every morning
- fed McDonald's every morning for breakfast
- fed Twinkies every morning for breakfast
- never fed breakfast

2. A four-year-old child who is:
- raised in a home without a substance-abusing adult
- sent to child care while his caregivers use drugs at home
- locked in his room at home while his parents use drugs
- left alone and locked in a car while his parents use drugs
- allowed to play and interact with his parents while they use drugs

3. A one-year-old child with ear infections who is:
- taken to the doctor when he shows signs of pain
- taken to the doctor after one week of waiting to see if symptoms pass
- given whiskey in his bottle to help dull the pain
- prayed over with no medical treatment
- not fed for one week to try to "starve" the symptoms

Some of the responses above are acceptable in virtually every community; others are unacceptable virtually everywhere. However, some of the responses may depend on community values. There is little doubt, though, that your own values also helped inform your choices.

Values and Child Neglect Self-Assessment

If you have ever said, "Well, I was _____ growing up, and I turned out just fine," you have made a values statement based on your own life history. Making a decision based on your own personal values code requires you to reference your own sense of right and wrong, your spiritual and political beliefs, and your own experiences. It is critical that you understand your own values as they relate to child neglect because, as a mandated reporter, you are required to report suspected child neglect based on community standards and your professional knowledge, not on your own values. As a professional, you must be cautious that your own values do not interfere with making an appropriate report. One way to do that is to take a values self-assessment. Use the checklist in Table 4.2 to explore your values related to child neglect.

Table 4.2 Values Self-Assessment

	Strongly agree	Agree	No opinion	Disagree	Strongly disagree
Children must never watch television before age two years.					
It is neglectful to feed a child fast food more than once a week.					
Babies should sleep in bed with their parents to encourage bonding and closeness.					
Children over age six years are competent to stay home alone for an hour.					
Parents who let their babies sit in dirty diapers for more than two hours are guilty of neglect.					
Poor families are more likely to neglect their children than middle-income families.					
It is inappropriate for babies to wear only simple "onesies" throughout their first year.					
Children should attend church every week.					
Parents should be sent to jail if they do not enroll their children in school.					
Obese children should be made to run every day.					
It is the right of a family to refuse lifesaving medical care for an infant.					
Infants should be allowed to cry themselves to sleep to make them more independent.					
Using small amounts of alcohol to help an infant through teething or colic is acceptable.					
Having dog feces on the floor where children play is a natural part of having a puppy.					
Withholding food from children is a meaningful way to make them learn.					
When parents force children to wear signs in public stating how they have misbehaved, it helps them learn.					
Giving a baby swimming lessons will allow you to let him or her swim alone safely for a few minutes without supervision.					

Handling Disclosure

Although preverbal infants and toddlers are the majority of neglected and fatally neglected children, older children, siblings, and even adults may verbally disclose neglect. This disclosure might be intentional or unintentional. When a child shares information that may indicate neglect, it is important to carefully hear what the child is saying and monitor your own reaction.

First, remain calm and accept what the child is saying without judgment. Be careful not to promise to keep a secret or start blaming adults. Avoid saying anything like "Your dad is a bad man for not feeding you, but I will take care of you now." A teacher might say instead, "It is my job to keep you safe. Sometimes I have to tell other adults so they can help keep kids safe." You may need to ask only enough open-ended questions to be sure you understand what the child is telling you. Remember that open-ended questions are those that cannot be answered by a mere yes-or-no response. An additional technique is to repeat the key words that the child uses. For instance, if a young child says, "Mommy locks me in the closet at night," you might repeat, "She locks you in the closet." This will encourage a child to keep talking so that you can establish suspicion.

Teachers should be cautious about asking too direct questions. Do not suggest any ideas to the child or offer an explanation or a rationale. Be sure to use only the child's own vocabulary. Remember, it is not your job to investigate. After you have visited with the child, you may want to make notes of exactly what the child has said. Avoid taking notes while you visit with the child; this can damage rapport and make the child feel like he or she is tattling. Include the time and date and any related information of which you may be aware, and then contact the authorities. When in doubt, make the report. You are responsible for reporting suspicion, not proof.

Quiz Me!

1. The reporting standard "should have known" refers to what?
   a. what teaching peers would agree is reportable
   b. what state law agrees is reportable
   c. what federal law agrees is reportable
   d. what a teacher's immediate supervisor agrees is reportable
2. In order to report, a teacher must have:
   a. physical evidence
   b. a child's disclosure
   c. proof
   d. suspicion
3. Which of the following might be an example of a behavioral indicator of neglect?
   a. a child who steals or hides food
   b. a child with physical or emotional developmental delays
   c. a young child who overly takes on the role of a parent
   d. all of the above
4. Diane DePanfilis has identified three levels of neglect. These include:
   a. fatal, nonfatal, and undetermined
   b. mild, moderate, and severe
   c. physical, emotional, and supervisory
   d. high, medium, and low
5. Those parenting practices that are generally accepted as appropriate in a geographic area are known as:
   a. values
   b. culture
   c. community standards
   d. minimally sufficient care
6. Should a child tell you that he or she "never eats breakfast," which of the following would be the best response?
   a. "I promise I won't tell anyone about this."
   b. "I don't eat breakfast either; that's OK!"
   c. "You never eat breakfast."
   d. "Sometimes parents can't feed their kids because they don't have any money; that's why we will feed you here at school if your mom will bring you on time."

7. A family who fails to secure a child in a car seat one time is engaging in _____ neglect, while a family who routinely leaves a child without a car seat is engaging in _____ neglect.
   a. moderate; severe
   b. nonfatal; fatal
   c. acute; chronic
   d. accidental; purposeful
8. True or false: Acute (one-time) neglect cannot be fatal.

Answers: a, d, d, b, c, c, c, false

Early childhood classroom life is deceptively complex. To an outsider, teaching young children looks easy, like play. But the exhausting reality is that teachers make hundreds of decisions each day. Teachers must make judgments that keep children physically and psychologically safe. They must understand the range of strengths and abilities among the group of

From the perspective of children and society, neglect is more important than abuse. We know neglect is more prevalent than abuse and less likely to be dealt with by child protective services. Harsh or abusive parenting is also generally less damaging than severe neglect in terms of cognitive and behavioral outcomes. (Wilson & Mullin, 2010).

children. They must try to engage and challenge each child where he or she is right now and help each child grow. Often teachers find themselves having to take action with little time to reflect beforehand. This has been described as "Ready . . . Fire . . . Aim." Although no one plans to take this approach, taking action without sufficient planning can be the result of the overwhelming demands placed on teachers each day. You can better prepare yourself to advocate for the children in your care by understanding your role in preventing, recognizing, and reporting child neglect. However, when it is time to report, you must be prepared to take that step.

It is normal to fear contacting child protective services. It is normal to fear sending the children home, where you believe their needs are not being met. It is normal to want to protect the children. The best thing that teachers and caregivers can do is to contact the appropriate authorities. In all states, if children are in immediate danger, the protocol is to dial 911 and protect them. However, when you suspect neglect but no imminent danger, it is time to contact your local child abuse prevention hotline (as listed in Appendix F). Remember that teachers are required to report suspicions; they are not required to confirm that neglect is happening. The agency will determine an appropriate response, investigation, and/or follow-up. Not only do we have to obey the laws about reporting child neglect, but we also have ethical responsibilities as early childhood professionals to follow the law and to protect children (NAEYC, 2005).

Teacher Fears

Teachers may feel uncomfortable reporting suspicions because they are not sure of the definition and signs of maltreatment, because they fear personal retaliation from the child's family, or because they are afraid that their suspicions may prove inaccurate. They also may fear that there will be retribution against the child or that the family will remove the child from the school. These are common concerns; however, no fear trumps the duty to protect a child.

When a teacher reports, the child protective services representative taking the call has been trained to collect the required information. This person is there to support the teacher in protecting a child and to help make the most accurate report possible. During a typical call, you will be asked to explain or describe your reason for calling. Report what you have seen, heard, or been told, and be sure to describe what has made you suspicious. These details along with any questions asked during the call will allow the representative to properly assess your report and prepare to respond.

Many teachers find support by consulting with each other or a supervisor prior to making a report. This can help a teacher sort out important information and may help other teachers recognize that they, too, need to report. Both teachers who have seen signs of neglect may wish to be present for the call, and both should insist that their names be connected to the report if they make a single report. It also can be advisable to make administrators aware of all potential problems; however, reporting to an administrator does not satisfy the requirement to report to child protective services.

It is important to note that not all reporting is a frightening, secretive experience. Part of your duty as a teacher or an administrator is to inform families at the outset of their time in your center of several things. For instance, your handbook should contain:

- a definition of child maltreatment;
- disclosure that all staff, volunteers, and other persons are mandated reporters of suspected child maltreatment (mandated reporting means that anyone who suspects child maltreatment is required by law to report it to appropriate authorities);
- the protocol for reporting.

Once families are aware of these circumstances, they may actually tell you about neglect in their own families as a means for asking for your assistance in reporting. Parents can be involved in making the call as a collaborative and caring effort and may ask for your assistance as they report suspected neglect for children who are not in your care. By making child protection a normal and healthy experience, you can help more children access needed resources.

"I Couldn't Believe It Worked"
I remember welcoming a new family to the center and going over our policies and procedures in our individual meeting, including our policy on reporting child abuse and neglect. The next time I saw the mother, she asked to meet with me privately and disclosed that after our meeting she realized that her sister and her husband were neglecting their own children. She reported that she had felt uneasy for a while, but it wasn't until our meeting that she realized she could do anything about it. She asked that I help her report; I called child protective services, explained that I was assisting a family in making a report, and then sat with her while she told her story. The experience really bonded me with that family and made me a believer in the importance of spending a few minutes educating every family about child maltreatment.

What You Need

Whether you are calling, consulting with a teacher about making a call, or helping a family report, it can be helpful to have a notepad with all of the child's information, including family information and details about the reason you are calling written down and in front of you. It is common to be nervous or to doubt yourself during a conversation with child welfare authorities, and this will help you be prepared. This can be an emotionally difficult time for you, but remember that your only job at this moment is to allow child protective services to determine if a child is safe. Your call could save a child's life.

Information required by authorities may include:

- Child's full name
- Address
- Telephone number
- Date of birth
- Child's developmental status (delays)

Also required may be:

- Parents' names
- Parents' address(es)
- Telephone number(s)
- Approximate ages
- Employers' names
- Employers' addresses
- Employers' telephone numbers
- Any emergency contacts listed with your facility

It is common for the authorities to ask questions such as:

- "Are there other adults or children living in the house?"
- "Do you know if there is any drug use in the house?"
- "Do you know if the family owns a gun?"
- "Do you have reason to believe that the family may run or hide from authorities?"
- "Does the family know you are making this call today?"
- "What is your relationship like with this family?"

"The First Time I Reported"

In my life, I have had to contact child welfare authorities many, many times. It never gets easier; I am just more prepared. The first time I had to call child welfare, I did what any good teacher does: I dialed the 1-800 number. It was busy for two days. Honestly, two full days! The child had come to school with a belt buckle imprint on his face. The family was new to the child care center I worked at, and I didn't know the mother at all. The child was three years old, the youngest of three children. The grandmother dropped the children off and picked them up, and the mother always paid in cash on Fridays. According to her enrollment card, she worked at Fancy's (some nail salon, I assumed). On the third day of calling the hotline, I finally got a person on the phone. I didn't have any information ready. I had to improvise and quickly look everything up in the computer. The agent on the phone asked when I first saw the belt buckle mark on the child's face, and I told him three days ago. The agent raised his voice and asked, "Why didn't you call 911?" I didn't know I was supposed to call 911. Why didn't someone answer the phone at the abuse hotline? An agent was in the child care center in less than two hours. The child's mark was still visible but, at this point, very faint. The agent scolded me and told me that in the future, if a child has visible marks, contact the police immediately. The agent interviewed the child. I had to help translate as the agent had trouble understanding a three-year-old with a speech impediment. He then made copies of the child's enrollment paperwork, which included his address, his parents' names, his date of birth, and his emergency contacts. The agent asked me where the mother worked. I responded, "Some nail salon." After looking at the card, he said, "Fancy's is a strip club, not a nail salon." He left and didn't take the children. However, that evening, he visited the children's home. The children came to child care the next day. They recounted how they received a visit from the police and DHS (the Department of Human Services). The oldest child, a boy, shared that this wasn't the first time they had had this type of visit. He also shared that this child care center was his third to attend in the past few months. On that second day after the DHS visit, the children never returned to the child care. My mind raced. "Did I do the right thing?" "Are they safe in their new center?" "If I hadn't called, would they still be here, in our center, now?" "Did the children receive another beating for my call?" This guilt will fade. What will always remain is the knowledge and feeling that I made a difference by calling child welfare. These children are now on the radar of child welfare authorities. They are a little bit stronger because someone stood up for them, and their abuser now knows that he or she is being watched.

Whose Job Is It?

In all states, there are mandated child abuse reporters. This means that teachers and other school personnel, social workers, physicians and other health workers, child care providers, medical examiners or coroners, and law enforcement personnel are required by law to contact local and/or state child welfare authorities and report suspected abuse or neglect. Most states operate a toll-free number for receiving reports, and all states allow anonymous reporting. However, it is helpful when callers provide their identity and contact information; this also allows the callers in some states to call and check back on the progress of the case. Child welfare workers may have questions later or need clarification, and contacting the original caller allows the agents to better care for the children in need. In general, the caller's identity is kept private and is not released to anyone, including the family being investigated.

For more information or for information specific to your state, visit www.childwelfare.gov. State requirements and statutes vary by state. For a list of statues or to review a summary of reporting laws for each state, visit the State Statutes Search section of Child Welfare Information Gateway's website at http://www.childwelfare.gov/systemwide/laws_policies/state/.

Quiz Me!

1. Families should be made aware of the definition of and policies regarding child neglect when:
   a. a report needs to be made
   b. they enroll at the center
   c. their child makes a disclosure
   d. they have a history of child protective services involvement

2. Consulting with another teacher prior to making a child protective services report is considered:
   a. illegal
   b. against child protective services policy
   c. helpful
   d. unethical

3. Which of the following is *not* needed for a child protective services report?
   a. child's developmental functioning
   b. child's address
   c. family's income
   d. your relationship with the family

4. Which of the following satisfies the mandatory reporting requirement for teachers?
   a. calling child protective services
   b. reporting to a principal or director
   c. confronting the family
   d. documenting until proof is established

5. A child who has experienced neglect may present as:
   a. distant and emotionally disinterested in you
   b. helpless
   c. aggressive
   d. all of the above

Answers: b, c, c, a, d

Thus far, we have discussed the forms and severity of child neglect, signs of neglect, and how to report suspicion. However, this is only one part of a teacher's responsibility. Child caregivers are at the front line for the prevention of child neglect and child-neglect fatalities, and parents, children, and teachers can all benefit from education, support, and modeling of best practices in child-neglect prevention and intervention.

By definition, prevention efforts are targeted at individuals who do not yet have the condition to be prevented—in this case, families who do not show signs of neglecting their children. Interventions are targeted for those who have some degree of symptoms of child neglect, have a history of child neglect, or present with risk factors for neglect or fatal neglect. While formal intervention is generally addressed through child protective services, child care providers can provide policies to support intervention efforts. In addition to prevention activities, additional strategies, such as the use of refferrals and resources, can be useful.

Prevention and Intervention Strategies to Provide to Parents

The first step in any prevention or intervention program is to develop a relationship with each family. When teachers get to know families, they have a sense of how family members relate to one another and the kinds of connections and supports they have with the community. When parents trust their child's teacher, they may be more likely to share what is happening in the child's life outside of school. Teachers can become more attuned to changes in a child's mood and behavior, especially when they are aware of new stresses on a family.

"My Grandparents Saved My Life"
I work at a petting zoo and am not expected to be able to work or support myself. That is because I suffered from brain damage when my parents gave me beer in my baby bottle. They didn't know better—they were just teenagers. My adoptive parents didn't listen to the doctors who told them what I wouldn't be able to do. They just expect me to do what I can. At first I volunteered at a camp for fourth and fifth graders, but they can be annoying, you know? I must've done a good job, though, because then they offered me this job. I really like working with little kids and taking care of the animals. My grandparents were brave to turn in their own child, so I could be adopted and have a better life.

Parent Handbook
Creating formal policies in the parent handbook that explain what neglect is, why children are or are not allowed to engage in certain behaviors, and the process for reporting neglect can help educate parents about issues of neglect. It is important that parents be informed about child neglect from the very start, as even a little knowledge can prevent some aspects of neglectful behavior. Specific efforts should be made at enrollment to review the handbook with parents and discuss child protection issues.

Parent Meetings/Trainings
Teachers can hold regular meetings or trainings on topics related to neglect and child safety. Teachers can present topics or recruit trainers from the community; additionally, some parents may wish to present as experts themselves. Nearly every month has an associated safety campaign, and child care facilities can capitalize on this by getting free resources for parent and child education. Bear in mind that improper supervision is the most lethal form of neglect, and even safety information that does not specifically mention neglect can be beneficial (see the chapter "Fatal Neglect").

Handouts
In addition to face-to-face meetings, information can be distributed through monthly handouts, blogging, or website posts. Some parents may even be interested in monthly e-mails about safety topics. The method of distribution is far less important than the fact

that it occurs. Usually if information is limited to once a month, this is a manageable amount. In lieu of handouts, however, your center may wish to produce a yearlong calendar that features different safety information each month, as well as important child care events. If you are very limited on resources, you can obtain many materials free for distribution.

Parent Library

The use of a parent lending library with books, pamphlets, DVDs or videos, CDs, or other materials can encourage parents to read about neglect topics on their own time. Centers may wish to consider incentives for parents to check out and use such materials. Incentives might include a twice-yearly drawing for a small gift card, available to all parents who check out and return materials.

Home Visitation

For some programs, annual or twice-yearly home visits are routine; for most centers, however, visits are not standard. The information gained in a home visit can be invaluable for assessing some types of neglect, such as environmental, deprivation of needs, or even supervisory. The most important role of the home visit, however, is to interact with the child in his or her own home, and it should never be promoted as a "dirty house" check. Be aware of cultural values involving gift giving, offerings of food and beverages, wearing shoes in the house, and any gender rules about who may and may not be left alone in the house together. If home visitation is to be used to build a relationship aimed at promoting healthy child development, then respect must be the foundation. The guidelines, expectations, duration, and activities of the home visit should be spelled out well in advance, as should the guidelines for reporting child neglect.

Resource Referrals

Encouraging family members to learn about resources before they need them is a major step in prevention. Many families will be unaware of systems to assist them with clothing, utilities, respite care, or food, and this can cost children dearly. It is important to make all families aware of these services because it is simply not possible to accurately assess a family's needs from a few minutes of visiting per day.

Parent Conferences and Active Listening

One of the greatest things a teacher can do to support a family is to listen, really listen, to what a parent or family member has to say and to do so without judgment. Active listening means hearing what a person has to say and letting him or her do most of the talking. When actively listening, you should give the parent your full attention with your posture and appropriate eye contact. Use small cues to help the parent keep talking, such as nodding or saying "mmm-hmmm," and avoid giving advice, especially before the parent has finished telling his or her story. Sometimes it just feels good to be heard.

In-Classroom Modeling

During drop-off and pickup, or other times at which family members visit the classroom, teachers can make extra efforts to verbalize how they supervise children. For example, teachers might point out how they have rearranged the furniture in the classroom so that they can supervise all children easily by sight and sound. They also might mention how large furniture has been tethered or removed to prevent tipping over.

Modeling at Parent Activities

During activities such as family picnics or other outings, teachers can demonstrate how they monitor children in nonschool settings. Teachers can discuss supervision plans with family members and can verbalize how they are supervising. An example might be a teacher who says to a group of parents, "I'm going to eat over here so that I can easily see if any children go near the edge of the lake. Water is fun, but such a hazard at this age."

Referrals to Authorities

Obviously, one of the best intervention strategies teachers have at their disposal is to report suspected neglect to child protection authorities. This will open doors to a variety of family support services. Remember that you have no way of knowing if your report is the first or the 50th; it could be the report that tips the scale in the favor of the child.

Accommodating Children's Therapies/Services

Teachers may need to consider that some services, such as developmental services, therapies, or parent observations, can best be held in the classroom or at the center. Being open to allowing these visits can help families better access services, decrease stress, and increase compliance.

Create Support Systems for Families

Families may be unaware of the services available to them, especially those new to the community and those who do not have strong English-language skills. Public libraries offer parenting classes and programs, as well as free programs for young children, and ethnic newspapers, and translated copies of local papers. Many churches and other organizations offer support groups for grief, single parenting, and other concerns such as raising children with special needs. Some communities offer directories of available services such as food pantries, clothing and housing assistance, and mental health services. In other communities, teachers will have to do some investigating. Schools might consider compiling lists of services available in the area for families of young children. This information could be included in newsletters, school handbooks, and a parent resource library.

Understanding Child Development

Parents need to have adequate knowledge of their child's development. Television programs and family members' own experiences or perceptions may give unrealistic expectations. We can teach parents what to expect at each stage of their child's development, covering topics that are common to most families, as well as those that are unique to just a few. We can help parents get to know their child individually through modeling, conversations, and providing information in parent meetings and newsletters.

Prevention and Intervention Strategies for Teachers

Staff Development Training

Teachers need to know what to look for and how to report suspected child neglect; directors may wish to consider requiring annual training in this area as part of continuing education requirements. Remember, too, that teachers can be perpetrators of neglect and fatal neglect, and their abilities to prevent this in their own classrooms must be continually developed. Professional development can focus on prevention strategies that provide support for families and children to lessen the likelihood of child neglect in the future. This may include teacher training on topics such as the following:

NURTURING

Children need to feel physically and emotionally secure. The way young children are treated changes their outlook on life. Positive, secure relationships between children and their teachers are fundamental for emotional development and crucial for learning and cognition (Nutbrown & Page, 2008). When children are abused or neglected, the brain's wiring is influenced in ways that affect a child's sense of self and social perception. Nurturing intervention can help rewire early damage. Both positive and negative early experiences shape the brain (Shonkoff & Phillips, 2000). As early childhood professionals, we need ongoing training in relating to children not only as a group, but also individually. We can play with children while they are alert and can take care of paperwork demands at naptime or after school. Focused attention is especially important for those who may not get enough nurturance outside our classrooms.

ENLARGING THE FRAME

The vast majority of elementary teachers are women, and 82.7 percent are white and non-Hispanic according to the National Center for Education Statistics. This indicates that the number of early childhood education teachers belonging to minority groups is diminishing. In addition to attracting a wider diversity of people into our profession, we need to enlarge our frame of reference and educate ourselves about the cultural experiences and expectations of the families we serve. We must understand that what is "normal" in our memories of childhood may be vastly different from the experiences of our students. This does not mean one is better; they are simply different. Engaging in meaningful cross-cultural training can improve our relationships with families.

Copple and Bredekamp (2009) describe a "both-and" approach when teachers and families have different goals for their children. For example, a parent may say, "I want you to spank my child if he acts up." Instead of shutting down the conversation by saying, "We don't do that," you might say, "It sounds like you want your child to be respectful and to pay attention. Those are my goals, too. Let me tell you about how we try to reach those goals at this school."

EMPOWERING PARENTS

As teachers, we must help parents to recognize the strengths in their own child and family, and to build upon those strengths. Parents may not know what to expect from their children at each developmental stage. Unrealistic expectations may lead them to believe that their children are capable of looking after themselves and their younger siblings before they are ready for such responsibility. Family members may view a child who cannot sit quietly for an hour or more as "behaving badly" when the child's behaviors are consistent with his or her age. When we help families to see the beauty and uniqueness of each child, despite any challenges and limitations, we build a foundation for more positive interactions.

Notes from the Field

"A Little Involvement Goes a Long Way"
Molly, a 19-year-old mother of Cherokee descent, presented as very shy and depressed. After a few weeks at the center, I asked her to demonstrate how to make fry bread for the preschool children. Nervous at first, she became very animated while sharing her expertise and family stories. This newfound confidence carried over through the rest of the year, as she began to volunteer to help with other projects and read to children and even teach us a little of the Cherokee language.

COMMUNITY RESOURCES

We believe that most people do the best they can in their given circumstances. Those circumstances may include consequences of poor choices such as substance addiction and incarceration, as well as problems with increased unemployment, reintegration for those returning from military service, and underemployment. It may be that generational cycles have left few apparent options. Additionally, the changing economy has resulted in decreased availability of social services, such as mental health treatment, child guidance services, and drug and alcohol treatment, and increased demand for such services including food banks and housing assistance. As teachers, we need to be well-trained in the availability of community services so that we can inform families about them. We want to empower families to become capable of handling a future crisis.

Prevention and Intervention Strategies in the Classroom

Classroom as a Safe Haven

For some children, school is the most predictable thing in their lives. When children's lives are filled with chaos and unpredictability, a calm teacher can be an anchor in a storm. Children feel confident and powerful in a classroom where they help create the rules. When children are given choices among projects, activities, and even books to read, they begin to trust their own judgment. Giving a child appropriate choices can defuse a heated exchange because the child feels the power to decide, rather than being forced into a solution that may seem unfair.

Comforting Routines

No matter a child's overall risk for neglect, the classroom can always be designed as a place in which children are well-supervised; emotionally, intellectually, and physically nurtured; and checked for signs of ill health. No child should ever experience neglect at school, and teachers need ongoing training in how to create a predictable and comforting environment. Children are comforted by a daily schedule posted on the wall, with photos or icons for nonreaders; by songs and stories on charts with illustrations children will recognize; and by having children's books in several areas around the room, corresponding to activity centers for children to look at and share with a teacher or friend.

Understanding Emotions

Feelings change. Children and even adults sometimes feel that what they are feeling right now will never change. This can lead to aggressive actions and depression. As a teacher, you can help children pause and examine their feelings throughout the day. "How do you feel right now? Do you remember how you felt when you came in this morning? What about when we got the hamster out?

Isn't it interesting how our feelings change?" Help children recognize and learn the names for all sorts of emotions, such as *frustrated, impatient, joyful, sleepy, eager, worried, calm,* and *scared.* When kids move beyond the basic *glad/happy, sad,* and *mad/angry,* they can think more carefully about what they are really feeling and what may have caused that feeling. They can learn to decide when they want to change feelings and learn ways to help that happen.

Self-Reliance

Classrooms should be set up so that children can take care of daily routines with little need to ask for help. Attendance and lunch count can be taken with magnetic or Velcro name tags, which the child can move to the appropriate column, or SMART Board or smart tablet sign-in sheets. Paper, markers, and scissors should be accessible to the children once safety routines have been taught. From the beginning, children should be taught to get materials out and put them away carefully to keep spaces safe and organized. Teachers can allow natural consequences; for example, when markers dry out due to loose lids, the class will not have markers to use for a while. Children with the fewest social skills are usually the ones who have the greatest need for positive social opportunities. Teachers have a huge impact on how a child is treated by others in the class. A teacher who models respectful ways to treat others and does not tolerate teasing and bullying will have a climate of acceptance in his or her classroom. We can provide a model through our behavior and can directly teach ways to invite others to play. We can role-play effective ways to ask to join a group. We can teach all children the importance of accepting people, valuing differences, and discovering the talents in everyone.

Bibliotherapy

According to the Bibliotherapy Education Project, a basic definition of *bibliotherapy* is "helping through books." Teachers can use quality literature to help children take another point of view, to feel connected to characters in the stories, and to imagine a variety of possible outcomes. This can be implemented formally by a trained clinician through clinical bibliotherapy to deal with significant problems, or informally by teachers and librarians or other laypeople through developmental bibliotherapy to facilitate normal development.

Comforting Children's Literature

A natural, easy way to provide comfort and support to all children is reading aloud. This can be done for the whole class at planned times but is even more effective when reading to a child or small group on a rug or comfy couch or chair. We have found the books listed in Table 6.1 to be favorites of children and teachers for their reassuring themes, soothing illustrations, and gentle rhythms.

Table 6.1 Comforting Children's Literature

Title and author	Description
Hug by Jez Alborough	As other jungle mothers cuddle their little ones, a little chimp desperately searches to give and receive a hug.
Grandfather Twilight by Barbara Berger	A magical, nearly wordless legend of beautiful illustrations that tell of a silent grandfather, his loyal dog, and a journey to deliver the moon into the sky.
Snuggle Puppy by Sandra Boynton	A sweet, singable celebration of unconditional love!
Goodnight Moon by Margaret Wise Brown	The classic tale of a young bunny's extended bedtime salutations.
Draw Me a Star by Eric Carle	A young artist creates a world of light and dark, sun and stars, all while exploring and pondering the cycle of life.
Today I Feel Silly and Other Moods That Make My Day by Jamie Lee Curtis	Fun rhymes make this an enjoyable exploration of common childhood feelings.
Time for Bed by Mem Fox	A lovely rhyme featuring close-up paintings of baby animals and their parents settling in for the night.
Wemberly Worried by Kevin Henkes	A thoughtful exploration of a young mouse's fears as she enters school and learns to make new friends.
What Comes in Spring? by Barbara Savadge Horton	An artfully woven tale of the changing seasons and one child's development.
Tell Me a Story, Mama by Angela Johnson	A precious tale of connecting generations through story and of belonging to a family.

Mama, Do You Love Me? by Barbara M. Joosse	A young Eskimo girl questions her mother's love. The mother beautifully describes in the Arctic setting how much and for how long her unconditional love will go on.
All the Places to Love by Patricia MacLachlan	A tender and beautiful story of being nurtured and learning to nurture as part of a family.
The Kissing Hand by Audrey Penn	A young raccoon is afraid to go to his first day of night school. His mother promises he will love school, but the potential for toys, friends, and new adventures will not convince the little raccoon to leave his mother. The mother raccoon shares her secret of the kissing hand, which will reassure the little raccoon through his school days and beyond.
What a Wonderful World by George David Weiss	A beautiful celebration of diversity.

Other beloved stories, such as those listed in Table 6.2, feature characters who envision new possibilities. They may spark conversations about patience, empathy, and the value of being unique.

Table 6.2 Empowering Children's Literature

Title and author	Description
Do You Want to Be My Friend? by Eric Carle	A wordless Eric Carle classic about connecting.
The Very Quiet Cricket by Eric Carle	With a delightful surprise at the end, Eric Carle gently reminds us that we will all shine when the time is right.
When I Was Little: A Four-Year-Old's Memoir of Her Youth by Jamie Lee Curtis	A charming story made rich with a child's own perspective on childhood.
The Crayon Box That Talked by Shane DeRolf	A clever presentation of the value of diversity.
The Magic Hat by Mem Fox	A bouncy rhyme featuring a mischievous wizard, some animal-like townsfolk, and a whimsical hat that seems to have a mind of its own.

Wilfrid Gordon McDonald Partridge by Mem Fox	An intergenerational tale of caring and connecting.
Chrysanthemum by Kevin Henkes	A caring and creative teacher helps a young mouse overcome teasing and serves as a model for celebrating uniqueness.
Sheila Rae, the Brave by Kevin Henkes	Even little sister mice can teach us a thing or two about true bravery.
Leo the Late Bloomer by Robert Kraus	Leo's father worries because he is not reading, writing, or speaking. Leo's mother, however, reassures him that Leo will do all those things and more when he is ready.
Jamaica Tag-Along by Juanita Havill	This story emphasizes empathy and perspective taking.
The Carrot Seed by Ruth Krauss	A timeless story of determination, hard work, and faith in yourself.
Tacky the Penguin by Helen Lester	A young penguin and his penguin friends discover the value of being different.
The Maggie B by Irene Haas	A beautifully illustrated tale of a young girl who lives out her fantasy of being both independent and nurturing as she sails across an imaginary sea in a boat named for her.
Fish Is Fish by Leo Lionni	A tadpole becomes a frog and returns to tell his minnow friend about life on land.
Uncle Jed's Barbershop by Margaree King Mitchell	A touching tale about pursuing dreams, no matter how long it takes.
The Rainbow Fish by Marcus Pfister	A beautifully illustrated story about sharing.
The Lamb and the Butterfly by Arnold Sundgaard	This story, with its beautiful illustrations by Eric Carle, demonstrates the variable nature of relationships.
I Love My Hair! by Natasha Anastasia Tarpley	A powerful tale encouraging pride in children's unique traits.
The Royal Raven by Hans Wilhelm	A tale of the true meaning of beauty, both inside and out.

"What I *Can* Do"

As an urban teacher, I eventually came to realize that I could not make everything "OK" for the children in my prekindergarten class. However, I did have a great deal of power over the six-and-a-half hours we were at school. I could make sure that there was food for hungry children to snack on and that families knew about school lunch and breakfast programs. I could make sure to have a stash of hats, socks, and gloves in the winter and underwear and a change of clothes for accidents year-round. I could make sure my classroom had Band-Aids, predictable routines, comforting songs and stories, and cozy places to work alone and with a friend. I could teach skills for peacefully resolving disputes, a love of stories, and how to find answers and ask questions.

A Safe Environment

At the most basic level, teachers need to create an environment that protects children from neglect in the classroom. Consider how your classroom, center, or home protects children against each of the following types of neglect:

Deprivation of needs: Do you provide nutritious food, spare clothing and shoes, and safe indoor and outdoor spaces?

Emotional: Do you model kind and positive language, relate to children in developmentally appropriate ways, and offer respect to each child and family?

Supervision: Is your environment safe from the hazards of neglect, such as bodies of water, unsecured doors and windows, fall hazards, and toxic chemicals?

Medical neglect: Are you aware of signs of illness or injury? Do you communicate these signs to parents, and do you have established emergency procedures for dealing with illness or injury?

Educational neglect: Do parents experience warmth and genuineness and learn to value education by interacting with you?

Environmental: Is your environment clean and safe? Is it free of clutter, food debris, and pet "accidents"?

My Report Card for Neglect Prevention and Intervention

Use the report card in Table 6.3 to score yourself on how well you have integrated neglect education for parents into your classroom.

Table 6.3 Report Card: Neglect Education for Parents

Prevention/Intervention Strategy	I do this with a focus on neglect. (A)	I do this in general, but not for neglect. (B)	I don't do this. (C)
Parent Handbook			
Parent Handouts			
Parent Meetings			
Parent Lending Library			
Home Visits			
Resource Lists/Guides			
Parent Conferences			
Making Reports			
Welcoming Services/Therapies			
Linking Families to the Community			
Providing Child Development Information			
Score:			

10–11 *A*s: You have a comprehensive neglect program; well done!

8–9 *A*s: You have a great foundation and are ready to expand into a few more areas.

7 or fewer *A*s: You have room to grow; your families need you!

"I'll Never Forget"

I remember an elementary teacher who, rather than punishing me for a minor infraction, said, "I expect better from you." She was the only model of an adult acting reasonably that I saw as a child living with abuse and neglect, and although she probably doesn't even remember the comment, I have worked my whole life to prove her right.

Quiz Me!

1. True primary prevention efforts are aimed at families who:
    a. have documented problems with neglect
    b. have no known problems with neglect
    c. are court-ordered
    d. none of the above

2. Intervention efforts include all of the following *except*:
    a. parent education
    b. home visiting
    c. teacher modeling
    d. removal from the center

3. Reviewing policies on safety and neglect from the parent handbook at the time of enrollment is important because:
    a. parents must give consent for you to report
    b. it is important for parents to be informed about expectations
    c. it is a legal requirement
    d. a signature is required to prove that you have done so

4. The first step in school-based prevention and intervention efforts is:
    a. building a relationship with the family
    b. obtaining informed consent from the family
    c. having a staff training on prevention and intervention
    d. deciding if you want to target neglect or abuse

5. Bibliotherapy:
    a. is a useful classroom tool for providing education, comfort, and prevention
    b. must be conducted by a librarian
    c. must be conducted by a licensed mental health professional
    d. is best used in conjunction with a home visitation program

Answers: b, d, b, a, a

"Child advocacy is speaking up for children who cannot speak for themselves. It is about speaking out on children's issues in public and working with policy makers behind closed doors, about introducing bold proposals to address long-standing challenges… A child advocate is motivated by a fierce belief that we, as a society, can do better for our children. And every day, every year, across America child advocates make a difference" (*Voices for America's Children*, 2006).

Advocacy comes in many forms. It can be speaking to a parent to help a child negotiate a situation. It can be a presentation to your colleagues or families. It can be volunteering for a neighborhood watch program. Advocacy takes on many forms from speaking one-to-one to speaking at a state government event. Advocacy is also speaking for those who cannot speak and for those who are afraid to speak. Advocates help identify a problem and a solution. They help educate those who need help and want change, and they ignite a fire in their communities to be better and do better. Advocacy is rewarding, invigorating, and exciting. It is also exhausting, emotionally draining, and sometimes scary.

Notes from the Field

"It's Just What I Do"
I am an everyday advocate. I am not trying to change "big government." I am not chasing abuse offenders down the street making citizen's arrests. I fight the good fight every day in my actions and genuine care and concern for my students.

Here are some examples of ways teachers can be everyday advocates:
- Share your life story and experiences with families. When parents see you as a person, they may come to you in times of need.
- Share with families what types of activities you and your children participate in class. Often they do not understand what is appropriate and what is not.
- Discuss mealtimes with families, such as what foods their child likes to eat at school. This conversation could open a door to proper nutrition for their child.
- Offer child-rearing trainings or classes after school and on weekends, and provide child care during those trainings/classes.

- Talk to your director or principal about working toward implementing more of the national standards for early childhood education, as well as developmentally appropriate practices (DAP) (Copple & Bredekamp, 2009).
- Walk your parking lot and playground every day to remove trash and dangerous items.
- Ask for volunteers. Model appropriate ways for family members who volunteer to communicate, discipline, and talk to their child.
- Talk to the families about their daily lives and social engagements. If families see you as more than a teacher, they are likely to confide in you. This relationship can stop or change the road to abuse and neglect.

Successful advocacy does not just happen, nor does it happen overnight. Successful advocacy is built on relationships. Just as government works on a system of networking and reciprocal favors, advocacy is a series of circumstantial networks and reciprocal favors. The key is relationships! Begin with the family members. When a new child enters your classroom or child care center, grab that opportunity to introduce and endear yourself to that family. Share a piece of your life with this family, open the door to communication, and see what happens. In most cases the family will reciprocate and share as well. This tiny, minute-long conversation is a moment of advocacy. Use this moment to build that relationship. A strong bond with a teacher or child care worker offers a stressed, in-need caregiver somewhere to turn for help. It also allows you as the teacher an opportunity to see the family in a new light. It allows you to understand the family's inner workings and nuances. Each family has its own beat, and it's our job as teachers to find that rhythm and plug into it. Find out what makes the family tick and what you have in common with the family members. How do you connect to their personal life? This connection not only will make you a better teacher but also will help you when times are rough.

"Uncomfortable Advocacy"

Many times in my career I struggled to connect with a family, but never more so than when I taught teen parents and their young children. At the time, I taught in a low socioeconomic high school outside a major city. For most of my students, I was their last chance to graduate high school. They were given to me because they were parents, and I was their last stop on a long road to being a high school dropout. I had almost nothing in common with my students or their parents. I was not a teen parent; I had my child at 29. I went to high school in a middle-class suburb. I did not struggle socially or academically in high school. I went to college successfully, then returned many years later to obtain a graduate degree. I grew up nowhere near my current job location but literally one thousand miles away. The only connection I had to these parents was that I, too, was a parent. I had never taught high school; I previously taught kindergarten or younger. Immediately, the students and parents knew I was a fish out of water. The first few months were challenging—mostly for me, as I struggled to communicate with young adults using my kindergarten-teacher vocabulary.

As you have worked through this book, we hope you have reached a new level of awareness about the seriousness of child neglect and that you feel empowered to identify it, prevent it, and report it. We hope you see yourself as an advocate as you buy dollar-store snacks and extra gloves to keep in your classroom. We hope you understand that your natural abilities to nurture, protect, and educate are the greatest weapons you have to fight child neglect. Most of all, though, we hope you have a permanent awareness that neglect is everywhere. If you have worked your way through this text, we can all but guarantee that you will begin to notice children around you who are experiencing neglect. This awareness can be a burden to your heart but a gift to the children you might save.

As you now decide what to do with the information you have read here, we encourage you to *act* as an everyday advocate by creating a plan to identify, prevent, and report suspected neglect and to *tell* others about the risks of neglect. It can be overwhelming to decide where to begin, so consider some of these techniques to help you remember the important talking points about neglect.

First, set a goal to talk to everyone about child neglect. How many times in a week does someone make small talk with you at the grocery store by asking, "What do you do?" or observing how good you are with children? This is a chance to name your occupation and then mention that you have a special interest in child neglect. You do not know when the person you are speaking to might be a policy maker, another teacher, or a family member who needs to hear this information. Ideally, you should be able to summarize the seriousness of neglect in less than one minute. As you go out into the world, remember that we all have a wish for child neglect to cease. We can all do this by remembering to be WISHERS:

Water: The number-one cause of death due to lack of supervision is drowning.

Infants: The younger the child is, the more likely neglect is to be fatal.

Supervision: Most children who die from neglect die because they are not appropriately supervised.

Harm: Harm can occur emotionally, intellectually, physically, socially, and through death.

Everyone: Neglect is present in all socioeconomic brackets, family types, and geographic locations.

Responsible: Any person who is responsible for watching a child can perpetrate neglect.

Six: There are at least six distinct ways in which children's basic needs can be neglected.

Second, be willing to train others. The materials in this book are designed to be used not only in the classroom but also in peer education. You are not the world's greatest speaker? That's OK! If a house were on fire and you were not a fireman, you would still call 911, right? With regard to child neglect, the house is on fire. Bring copies of the handouts from this book and let a discussion happen. Any discussion is better than no discussion.

Third, be an effective model for appropriate care, interactions, and supervision. The choices you make in your own classroom or child care facility serve not only as a primary way to keep children safe, healthy, and nurtured but also as a way to educate others about safe and nurturing choices. Your behavior, classroom structure, and policies can demonstrate that kindness and nurturing are not options but are requirements for producing healthy children. You can demonstrate that appropriate nutrition choices, clothing options, and attention to children's physical complaints is a necessary part of child caregiving. Finally, you can demonstrate appropriate supervision practices, any one of which can prove lifesaving. To do this, be comfortable about inviting family members and administrators into your room to see your strategic plan for preventing child neglect and meeting the totality of children's physical, intellectual, and emotional needs.

111th Congress, Senate. 2010. CAPTA reauthorization act of 2010. Report 111-378. Accessed on April 10, 2013. http://www.gpo.gov/fdsys/pkg/CRPT-111srpt378/pdf/CRPT-111srpt378.pdf.

American Academy of Pediatrics (1997). "Religious objections to medical care." *Pediatrics*, 99(2), 279-281.

American Psychological Association. 2012. *Postpartum depression.* Accessed October 11, 2012. www.apa.org/pi/women/programs/depression/postpartum.aspx.

Barth, Richard P. 2009. "Preventing child abuse and neglect with parent training: Evidence and opportunities." *The Future of Children,* 19(2), 95–118. Accessed June 8, 2011. www.futureofchildren.org.

Bonner, Barbara L., Mary Beth Logue, Keith L. Kaufman, and Larissa Niec. 2001. "Child maltreatment". In C. Eugene Walker and Michael Roberts, eds. *Handbook of Clinical Child Psychology*, 3rd ed. New York: John Wiley & Sons.

Brett, Kate, Wanda Barfield, and Cheryl Williams. (2008). "Prevalence of self-reported postpartum depressive symptoms—17 states, 2004-2005." *Morbidity and Mortality Weekly Report*, 57(14). Centers for Disease Control and Prevention.

Bronfenbrenner, Urie. 1976. *The Ecology of Human Development.* Cambridge, MA: Harvard University Press.

Chan, Yuk-chung, Gladys L.T. Lam, and Wan-Chae Shae. 2011. "Children's views on child abuse and neglect: Findings from an exploratory study with Chinese children in Hong Kong." *Child Abuse & Neglect,* 35, 162–172.

Childhelp. 2012. *Prevention and Treatment of Child Abuse.* Accessed October 13, 2012. www.childhelpusa.org.

Copple, Carol, and Sue Bredekamp, eds. 2009. *Developmentally appropriate practice in early childhood programs serving children from birth through age eight*. 3rd ed. Washington, DC: National Association for the Education of Young Children.

Crittenden, Patricia, and Mary Ainsworth. 1989. "Child maltreatment and attachment theory." In Dante Cicchetti and Vicki Carlson, eds. *Child maltreatment: Theory and research on the causes and consequences of child abuse and neglect.* 432–463. New York: Cambridge University Press.

Crosson-Tower, Cynthia. 2003. *"The role of educators in preventing and responding to child abuse and neglect."* U.S. Department of Health and Human Services Administration for Children and Families, Administration on Children, Youth and Families, Children's Bureau Office on Child Abuse and Neglect. Accessed June 1, 2011. http://www.childwelfare.gov/pubs/usermanuals/educator/educatorg.cfm.

Department of Transportation's National Highway Traffic Safety Administration (2010). Accessed on June 18, 2012. http://www. distraction.gov/content/press-release/2011/12-8.html.

DePanfilis, Diane. 2006. *Child neglect: A guide to prevention, assessment, and intervention.* Washington, DC: U.S. Department of Health and Human Services.

DePanfilis, Diane, and Howard Dubowitz. 2005. "Family connections: A program for preventing child neglect." *Child Maltreatment,* 10(2), 108–123. Accessed June 5, 2011. http://cmx.sagepub.com/content/10/2/108.

Dubowitz, Howard, and Maureen M. Black. 2001. "Child neglect." In Robert M. Reece and Stephen Ludwig, eds. *Child abuse: Medical diagnosis and management.* 2nd ed. 339–362. Philadelphia: Lippincott, Williams & Wilkins.

Dubowitz, Howard, Jeongeun Kim, Maureen Black, Cindy Weisbart, Joshua Semiatin, and Laurence Magder. 2011. "Identifying children at high risk for a child maltreatment report." *Child Abuse & Neglect,* 35, 96–104.

Duva, Joy, and Sania Metzger. 2010. "Addressing poverty as a major risk factor in child neglect: Promising policy and practice." *Protecting Children,* 25 (1). Accessed April 10, 2013. http://aia.berkeley.edu/media/2011_teleconferences/poverty/Protecting%20Children%20Article%20on%20Poverty%20and%20Neglect.pdf.

Earls, Marian. 2010. "Clinical report: Incorporating Recognition and Management of Perinatal and Postpartum Depression Into Pediatric Practice." *Pediatrics,* 126(5), 1032-1039.

Farmsafe. 2003. *Child safety on farms, Factsheet 2: Child Development and Risk.* www.farmsafe.org.au/index.php?id=53.

Hoffman-Plotkin, Debbie, and Craig Twentyman. 1984. "A multimodal assessment of behavioral and cognitive deficits in abused and neglected preschoolers." *Child Development,* 35, 794–802.

Howard, Kimberly S., and Jeanne Brooks-Gunn. 2009. "The role of home-visiting programs in preventing child abuse and neglect." *The Future of Children,* 19(2), 119–146. Accessed June 13, 2011. www.futureofchildren.org.

Katz, Karyn. 1992. "Communication problems in maltreated children: A tutorial." *Journal of Childhood Communication Disorders,* 14(2), 147–163.

Kemple, Krixten, and Hae Kyoung Kim. 2011. "Suspected child maltreatment: Recognize and respond." *Dimensions of Early Childhood,* 39(2), 2011.

Klevens, Joanne, and Rebecca T. Leeb. 2010. "Child maltreatment fatalities in children under 5: Findings from the national violence death reporting system." *Child Abuse & Neglect,* 34(4), 262–266.

Lawrence, Ruth, and Penelope Irvine. 2004. "Redefining fatal child neglect." *Child Abuse Prevention Issues,* 21. Accessed June 11, 2011. http://www.aifs.gov.au/nch/pubs/issues/issues21/issues21.html.

Mennen, Ferol E., Kihyun Kim, Jina Sang, and Penelope K. Trickett. 2010. "Child neglect: Definition and identification of youth's experiences in official reports of maltreatment." *Child Abuse & Neglect,* 34, 647–658.

National Association for the Education of Young Children. 2003. *Building Circles, Breaking Cycles: Preventing child abuse and neglect*. Washington DC: NAEYC.

National Association for the Education of Young Children. 2005. *Code of ethical conduct and statement of commitment: A position statement of the National Association for the Education of Young Children*. Accesses on June 15, 2012.
http://www.naeyc.org/files/naeyc/file/positions/PSETH05.pdf.

National Center for Education Statistics. (n.d.). *Table 2. Percentage distribution of school teachers, by race/ethnicity, school type, and selected school characteristics: 2007–08*. Accessed October 26, 2012.
http://nces.ed.gov/pubs2009/2009324/tables/
sass0708_2009324_t12n_02.asp.

National Children's Advocacy Center. 2012. Accessed October 13, 2012.
http://www.nationalcac.org.

NSW Child Death Review Team (1999), *1997-1998 Annual Report*, NSW Commission for Children and Young People, Sydney.

NSW Child Death Review Team (2000a), *1998-1999 Annual Report*, NSW Commission for Children and Young People, Sydney.

NSW Child Death Review Team (2000b), *1999-2000 Annual Report*, NSW Commission for Children and Young People, Sydney.

NSW Child Death Review Team (2001), *2000-2001 Annual Report*, NSW Commission for Children and Young People, Sydney.

NSW Child Death Review Team (2002), *2001-2002 Annual Report*, NSW Commission for Children and Young People, Sydney.

Nutbrown, Cathy, and Jools Page. 2008. *Working with babies and children from birth to three*. London: Sage.

Owens, Karen B. 2002. *Child and adolescent development: An integrated approach*, Wadsworth/Thomas Learning: Belmont, CA.

Perry, Bruce D. 2005. "The power of early childhood." Paper presented at Kansas Health Foundation 2005 Leadership Institute.

Polansky, Norman A., Carolyn Hally, and Nancy F. Polansky. 1975. *Profile of neglect: a survey of the state of knowledge of child neglect*. Washington, DC: U. S. Department of Health, Education, and Welfare.

Safe Kids USA. 2009. *Safety fact sheets*. Accessed October 13, 2012.
www.safekids.org/our-work/research/fact-sheets/.

Self-Brown, Shannon, Kim Frederick, Sue Binder, Daniel Whitaker, John Lutzker, Anna Edwards, and Jaimi Blankenship. 2011. "Examining the need for cultural adaptations to an evidence-based parent training program targeting the prevention of child maltreatment." *Children and Youth Services Review*, 33, 1166–1172. Accessed June 1, 2011.
www.elsevier.com/locate/childyouth.

Shonkoff, Jack, and Deborah Phillips (eds). 2000. *From Neurons to Neighborhoods: The Science of Early Childhood Development*. National Research Council and Institute of Medicine. Washington, DC: National Academy Press.

Slack, Kristen Shook, Lawrence M. Berger, Kimberly DuMont, Mi-Youn Yang, Bomi Kim, Susan Ehrhard-Dietzel, and Jane L. Holl. 2011. "Risk and protective factors for child neglect during early childhood a cross-study comparison." *Children and Youth Services Review*, 33, 1354–1368.

Stagner, Matthew W., and Jiffy Lansing. 2009. "Progress toward a prevention perspective." *The Future of Children*, 19(2), 19–38. Accessed June 8, 2011. www.futureofchildren.org.

Stiffman, Michael N., Patricia G. Schnitzer, Patricia Adam, Robin L. Kruse, and Bernard Ewigman. 2002. "Household composition and risk of fatal child maltreatment." *Pediatrics*, 109(4), 615–621.

Trentham, Bart. 2007. "The school's role in the intervention of child abuse and neglect." Child Abuse Training and Coordination Program, Family Support & Prevention Service, Family Health Service, Oklahoma State Department of Health. Accessed June 5, 2011. http://www.ok.gov/health2/documents/School%20Reporting%20Manual%2007.pdf.

Wolock, Isabel, and Bernard Horowtiz. 1984. "Child maltreatment as a social problem: The neglect of neglect." *American Journal of Orthopsychiatry*, 54 (4), 530-543.

University of San Diego School of Law. 2012. *Children's Advocacy Institute*. Accessed October 13, 2012. http://www.caichildlaw.org.

U.S. Department of Health and Human Services (n.d.). "Preventing child abuse and neglect." Accessed June 5, 2011. www.childwelfare.gov.

The Reauthorization of the Child Abuse Prevention and Treatment Act (CAPTA): Hearing Before U.S. Senate Committee on Health, Education, Labor and Pensions, Subcommittee on Children and Families. June 26, 2008. (statement of Dr. Cheryl Anne Boyce, Chief, Child abuse and neglect program, National Institutes of Health) Accessed June 5, 2011. http://www.hhs.gov/asl/testify/2008/06/t20080626a.html.

U.S. Department of Health and Human Services. 2012. State Laws on Child Abuse and Neglect. https://www.childwelfare.gov/systemwide/laws_policies/state/can.

Voices for America's Children. 2006. *Voices for America's Children*. Accessed October 13, 2012. http://www.voices.org.

Wilson, Philip, and Anne Mullin. 2010. "Child neglect: What does it have to do with general practice?" *British Journal of General Practice*, 5–7.

Child Care Self-Assessment: Prevention Efforts

Use this checklist to assess the kinds of prevention and intervention services you are aware of, as well as the ones you actively make families aware of. We suggest completing this checklist at the beginning of this book, and again at the end. Use the "Other" line to include other efforts you make that are not listed here.

I am AWARE of these services.	I make FAMILIES aware of these services.	
		NEGLECT AREA: DEPRIVATION OF NEEDS
		Food banks
		Free meal services
		Coupons for food/cleaning supplies
		Home safety information
		Bill assistance services
		Other:
		NEGLECT AREA: MEDICAL NEGLECT
		Medical appointment transportation services
		Public insurance programs
		Medication safety information
		Immunization schedules
		Public health services/health department
		Other:

I am AWARE of these services.	I make FAMILIES aware of these services.	
		NEGLECT AREA: SUPERVISORY NEGLECT
		Ages and stages guidelines for supervision
		Information on choosing a safe babysitter
		Treatment information for drug/alcohol abuse
		Information on respite care
		Specific information on common safety hazards
		Other:
		NEGLECT AREA: EDUCATIONAL NEGLECT
		Transition issues between preschool and public school, including required documentation
		Center rules for attendance hours, days, and absences
		Other:
		NEGLECT AREA: ENVIRONMENTAL NEGLECT
		Car seat availability and car seat checks
		Room-by-room safety checklists for the home
		Information on food safety
		Information on pet safety
		Other:
		NEGLECT AREA: EMOTIONAL NEGLECT
		Guidelines for discipline and guidance for different ages
		Feeding guidelines for infants
		Other:

Ask the Experts: Case Studies for Review and Discussion

Read each of the following cases, and answer the questions. After you have responded, take a look at the responses written by active classroom teachers. How do your answers compare?

Case 1

Jake is a 17-month-old child who has been in the care of your center for three months. You have noticed that he tends to wear the same outfits again and again. Lately, you have noticed that he will wear the same one for several days in a row, and it does not appear to be cleaned between wearings. Additionally, Jake generally presents to your class in an already heavily soiled diaper. You suspect that perhaps he is not being changed upon awakening in the morning. When he first started in your program, his mother would do all the dropping off and picking up; however, over the last month Jake has been dropped off by at least five different people. His mother explains that she is required to do shift work and has had a temporary change to the daytime (6 a.m. to 2 p.m.) shift. She still picks him up every day. The people who are dropping Jake off are generally unable to answer any questions about him, such as "How did he sleep?" or "Is he feeling well today?" They tend to hand him over quickly and depart without a goodbye, which Jake does not protest. On one occasion, the person dropping him off sent him into the center with a six-year-old to take him to your class.

Do you suspect any neglect in this scenario? Which types?

What action, if any, would you take at this point for Jake, his mother, his substitute caregivers, the school, or the public human services agency?

How would your answers change if one of the people dropping him off smelled strongly of alcohol one morning?

Case 1: Responses

RESPONSE 1

I would suspect physical neglect but probably some emotional neglect as well. First, I would make sure to document everything. Next, I would speak to Jake's mother to find out as much as possible about the situation. I would ask for information about those bringing Jake and ask for her impressions of those people. If no one has already spoken to the mother about the way he is being brought to the center, it should be done immediately so the mother has the chance to make corrections. If her responses are not adequate and if no corrections are made in Jake's physical condition, I would report the situation to the human services agency.

If I smelled alcohol on the person dropping Jake off, I would contact the human services agency immediately.

RESPONSE 2

First, I would make sure the family knows I am there to listen. I would try to understand the challenges the family members are facing and locate appropriate services in the community to help them find support. I want to know them in their "life-world" beyond the classroom and develop a climate of trust over time. A teacher I once worked with actually marked a diaper with a marker dot in order to confirm that the child was arriving at school in the previous afternoon's diaper. This discovery caused her to contact authorities, who discovered complicated divorce arrangements and a father who was overwhelmed. He and his family truly benefitted from the subsequent required parenting classes.

I have known teachers and directors who have "accidentally lost" an intoxicated-appearing parent's keys and shared coffee and conversation while the keys were being hunted, to allow the parent to sober up before driving home. Another choice would be to call the police.

Case 2

Molly is an eight-month-old infant who presents to child care every day wearing a stained white "onesie" and no other clothing. This has been true for the three months you have kept her. It does not appear to be the same outfit every day, but each set of clothing is dirty. You know that Molly lives with her mom, her mom's boyfriend, her grandmother, and two older siblings, so you assume that one of the adults or older children should be able to get her dressed appropriately. Her nose is frequently crusty, her face is dirty, and her hair is never combed or neatly styled with a bow, unlike many of the other female infants. Molly has run out of diapers at school, and you find yourself feeling irritated that her mother cannot remember to bring them despite frequent requests. The family drives an older-model luxury car, but in actuality, you are unsure of the family's financial situation.

What other information, if any, would you want to gather before deciding if this is neglect or not?

How do your own values influence your opinion on this case?

Imagine that you phone child protective services and make a report; you later follow up and learn that the case was closed without intervention. What types of prevention or intervention could you provide at your center to address your concerns?

Case 2: Responses

RESPONSE 1

Before deciding if this was neglect, I would want to know the reason the mother has not provided diapers. In addition, I would want to make sure the clothing is actually dirty and not just stained. While one of my values is that it is the job of adults to care for children, I am not as sensitive to dirty faces or runny noses as others I know. However, the fact that the mucus is crusty is a concern to me, likely because it signals a longer-term lack of care. I think that even with infants, some people have different expectations for girls and boys, and this bothers me. Hence, not having a bow is not a problem for me, nor is not having her hair combed.

Other types of prevention or intervention we could provide at the center include making sure Molly goes home each day with a clean face. We could also wash her "onesie" that day and subsequent days to find out if it is actually dirty or just stained. We could also offer some other "onesies," explaining to the mother that these are extras that had been left. We could also speak directly to the mother about ways to get Molly ready each day and offer any assistance if she has questions.

RESPONSE 2

Chronic and crusty runny nose might indicate allergies, which might indicate substandard housing with mold or other hazards. I would want to get to know the members of the family, find out where they are living, and see if they are aware of other housing options. Then I would want to make sure they know about the availability of health insurance for children. I would make sure the family is aware of the clothing closet at our school and the food banks sponsored by area churches each week. These conversations would likely be awkward, and could be offensive if I have not already established a relationship with the family. This family needs to know that we are here to care for each other, not to judge or dismiss.

Case 3

One of your most involved parents, Stella, who is the mom of two children in your center ages three and five, attends a yearly parent–teacher conference to discuss the progress of her youngest child. Stella has always been very active and friendly, and you respect her parenting style. During this conference, she discloses to you that the family has been struggling financially. She states that she and her husband both have had to take on shift work, which requires her to leave the house at 5 a.m., while her husband is unable to return home until 7 a.m. They have been leaving their two daughters home alone, asleep, during this two-hour gap. She states that she hates doing it, but the family cannot afford for either parent to quit. She asks if you have any suggestions on how she can make her five-year-old more responsible to care for the three-year-old, in case she wakes up.

What is your response to this case?

What type of neglect is present here, if any? Would you classify it as mild, moderate, or severe?

What type of conversation would you want to have with Stella?

Case 3: Responses

RESPONSE 1

I am concerned for the safety of the children; neither is of an age that I would consider competent to handle an emergency like a fire alarm or a burglar. I think the parents are well intentioned and probably in a bit of a spot, but I do think it is neglect because the children do not have an adequate supervisor. I might consider it moderate because, although nothing has happened yet, the potential for something to happen (and for that something to be very, very bad) is very real.

I would absolutely talk to Stella about how this may be both her best option *and* an unsafe option. I would let her know that because there is the potential for grave harm to befall the children, I must call child protective services. I would really work to reassure her that I am not punishing her, nor will I advocate for her to temporarily lose custody of her children. I would let her know that I respect that she is doing the best that she can, but that if we call child protective services, we can get her in line for additional services that might allow her to change jobs, adjust her schedule, or access early-morning care. I would want Stella to make the phone call with me to preserve the relationship that I have with her so that we can continue to work together in the best interests of the child. After the call, I might even explore more options with her, like seeing if I can help her identify an affordable sitter for those early-morning hours. Definitely report.

RESPONSE 2

I would classify this as severe neglect because in the worst-case scenario, pipes could burst, there could be a fire, or either child could wake up disoriented and wander out of the house and into traffic or a pool while looking for his or her parents. I would help the mother understand that this is a very dangerous thing to do. I would suggest alternatives like before-school drop-off with a neighbor, relative, or classmate. If she seems at all hesitant to change arrangements, I would contact child protective services immediately.

Case 4

There is a mother who has a three-year-old child, Antoine, in your center. She routinely presents to pick this child up with two older children who appear to be about six and eight years old. Antoine says that these children are his "bubby" and "sissy." One day while visiting during pickup time, you make a remark to the oldest child about how early he must get out of school and how nice it is that he can come pick up his little brother. He looks down and tells you that he does not go to school. His mother looks uncomfortable and quickly leaves with the children. The next day, she asks to speak to you privately and discloses that she has not put her older children in school this year because the family's utilities were cut off, and she was told by the public school secretary that she could not enroll the children without an electric bill to prove residency. The children have not been in school for five months, and the family has not had electricity throughout this time. You are shocked and realize you have never suspected the problems this family might be having.

Is neglect present in this case? If so, what type?

Discuss the type of intervention services you would want to provide. Are there prevention services that you think might have been useful in this situation?

Case 4: Responses

RESPONSE 1

This is a sad case, but one I know is very real. I do think this is educational neglect and may also be environmental neglect, depending on the circumstances under which the children are living without power. I wonder what else they are doing without, like food or medicine. There is potential for many forms of neglect here, but definitely educational and probably environmental.

I would let the mother know that I am very concerned but that I am also grateful that she has trusted me with this information. I would also let her know that I want to try to advocate for her and her children by phoning child protection, possibly calling the school to find out what options there are for children who lack that type of documentation (I would think there must be an alternative!), and making sure that I listen to and respect her.

From a prevention standpoint, it would have been nice to have information about transition to public schools, utility assistance, options for home- or web-based schooling, and other necessary services available in the center for all to use.

RESPONSE 2

I would make time to have a longer visit with this parent and find out if the family has been living for months without electricity. I would have names and contact information for community agencies that could provide adequate housing, utility bill assistance, and other aid the family might need. I would also contact the homeless liaison at the local school district and try to arrange a meeting with this family to share other resources that may be available such as transportation, federal food programs, and so on. Although many districts say they require a utility bill or birth certificate for attendance, an attorney and national advocate for the homeless stated in a workshop that these policies are against federal law. If the family is unwilling to enroll the children in school and is not homeschooling them, I would report the truancy to the local school district.

Case 5

You have been working with the Hernandez family for several years and currently serve the third of the family's three children. Both parents have always been very positive, encouraging, and involved. However, you become concerned because they seem to have a very different relationship with their youngest child than they did with their first two children. You observe that the mother rarely smiles or attends to the youngest baby, now age six months. She appears to ignore his needs and cries and is quick to put him down at drop-off. She will actively move away from him as he reaches for her and will remove his hands from her if he touches her. You have observed her rolling her eyes and sighing in frustration when he attempts to get her attention, and you have never heard her use the baby's name. Instead, she regularly calls him "the little jerk" and "my little life sucker." The mother rarely smiles at all anymore, seems to move slowly, and generally looks unhappy.

What is your assessment of this case as it relates to potential neglect?

What actions would you take?

Case 5: Responses

RESPONSE 1

I would be extremely worried about emotional neglect in this case; this mother seems to be depressed and unable to engage with her baby. The first year is so important for building a healthy attachment that I would be very concerned that he is not getting what he needs from her. I would certainly want to make note of the baby's height and weight as well, because this type of emotional neglect could be related to failure to thrive and the baby could be starving to death.

I would very gently and privately talk to this mom and let her know that I have noticed some major changes. I would want to hear her talk about what is going on, and if she herself thinks she is depressed. I would also want to find out if she is receiving counseling or medication or if she perceives that there are barriers such as cost that would keep her from getting these services. I would really want to hear her full story about other stressors that may be going on as well and let her know that I am going to phone child protective services to try to initiate some help on her behalf.

RESPONSE 2

I would be concerned about the apparent rejection of this child and worry about his emotional needs being met. I would also worry about maternal depression. I would gather as much information as possible through conversation, empathize with the stresses of motherhood, and try to connect this mother with respite care and other community services. I would ask her to talk to her physician about depression. I would also provide extra nurturing and attention to the child while in my care and model appropriate interactions. I would take special care to point out his capabilities and accomplishments.

Case 6

A new family enrolls in your center. The parents have a 14-month-old, Jeremiah, and a 36-month-old, Susan. On the first day of school, they fail to show up with any of the required infant supplies for Jeremiah, such as diapers, wipes, and snacks. When you ask, they report to you that he is fully toilet trained and will not be wearing diapers. They instead request that you simply place him on the toilet every 45 minutes. If he has an "accident," the parents state that they give him two smacks with a hand on his bare bottom and say, "Naughty!" They understand that you do not allow spanking at your center but still want him placed on the toilet regularly. They report that they did this same method with their older child and it worked well.

You consult with your director, who discloses to you that there is some difficulty with Jeremiah's older sister, as well. She reportedly has an extremely red and painful-appearing diaper rash. Her parents said that it will go away and was merely the result of Susan refusing to use the toilet over the weekend. Her father stated, "She didn't want to go, so we put her in a diaper like a baby and let her sit in it. We even had to duct tape it on!" He laughed at this but stated, "I don't think she'll refuse to go in the potty again after that!"

What is your response to this case?

What type of neglect do you suspect, and what level would you classify it as?

What type of intervention and prevention might you use?

Case 6: Responses
RESPONSE 1

I would have a meeting with the parents and the director of the facility to determine the correct way to handle the situation and any possible options that we could assist with that would be more appropriate for toilet training. I would also have to contact the child abuse hotline and report the case to the department of health services or child protective services.

I feel this would be classified as physical and mental abuse of the children. In my opinion, any type of abuse is severe, especially when the well-being of the children is at stake, which seems to be the situation in this case. Although child protective services is not always reliable, I would have to follow the right chain by starting with the professionals from this organization first and allowing them to take over the case as they see fit. Parenting programs could be an option, too.

RESPONSE 2

As this case involves a new family, there has likely been little chance to establish any rapport. I would try to remain calm and explain that a child of three years isn't capable of such long-term generalizations, and that both children may not have the physical development to control elimination. I would hope to have the courage to then explain that as a mandatory reporter, it would be against the law if I didn't report this suspected abuse. In reality, I would probably be afraid that the parents would yell at me or take their children and never return, so I would likely wait for them to leave, then call child protective services. I would ask the director to be present while I took photos of the rash, and I'd write down exactly what the parents had said and share that with the caseworker.

Parenting classes that emphasize child development might be the perfect solution.

Case 7

Marly is an 18-month-old toddler who has enrolled in your center. During enrollment, her mother disclosed that she has cystic fibrosis and requires both enzymes and breathing treatments during the day. Initially, you were provided with information and physician instructions on what to do. However, within a few weeks, Marly's family stops bringing the needed supplies. You ask, confidentially, if her treatment regimen has changed. Her mother pauses and then tells you that she and her husband have decided that they want Marly to not be different from her peers. They are planning to not bring any more enzymes to school and to only do interventions at home at night. You suspect this is against medical advice and fear this choice may have dire consequences for Marly's well-being.

What steps will you take right away in this case?

Discuss the type(s) of neglect you suspect.

How can you advocate for this family?

Case 7: Responses

RESPONSE 1

First, I would let Marly's parents know that her treatment can be given privately and that confidentiality is being upheld. Then I would ask for a physician's note that it is OK to skip the afternoon treatment. Also, in a conference with my director, I would explain how much her peers would be getting out of the experience, as well as Marly. It is good to expose children to all types of differences, as that's how they learn compassion and empathy. Her peers could be a part of the process of her therapy, and each would learn a great deal. Focus on the importance of inclusion. Offer articles on what children get out of being in an inclusive class.

RESPONSE 2

I would suspect medical neglect. I would call child protective services right away and hope a representative would contact the physician. I would talk to the parent about how the care is handled discreetly at school, to provide privacy and avoid embarrassment. I would then share my concerns about the child's well-being. I would further share about my own child's special needs and help the parent understand that all children have individual needs and that addressing each child's individual needs is much more "fair" than treating everyone the same way.

Sample Reporting Form: Making the Call

Use this form to help collect your thoughts and observations and to give yourself the courage to report suspected maltreatment. Remember: You do not have to *know*; you only have to *suspect*.

Child's full name:	
Reporter's Address:	
Reporter's Telephone number:	
Child's Date of birth/age:	
Is child developmentally delayed?	
Parent(s) name(s):	
Child's address:	
Parent(s) phone number:	
Parent(s) workplace (if known):	
Parent(s) daytime contact information:	
Emergency contacts:	

Why are you calling?	suspect:	abuse	neglect	both
If neglect, what kind(s)?				
Is the child safe now?				
Do the parents know you are calling?				
Are there other adults or children living in the house?				
Do you know if there is any drug use in the house?				
Do you know if the family owns a gun?				
What is your relationship like with this family?				
What made you suspect maltreatment?				
I *saw*:				
I was *told*:				
Other signs and symptoms:				
Important dates/times:				

Parent Pages

The following original parent handouts were designed specifically for this book to provide an easy, once-a-month set of neglect prevention information that can be used by teachers and directors. Many of the handouts correspond to a national safety month; however, you are free to distribute them in any order you wish. Remember that, although the handouts can stand alone, they may be most effective in combination with parent meetings, trainings, and other education efforts.

Early Development and the Brain

THE FACTS
- The first three years of a baby's life account for explosive brain growth, with hundreds of trillions of brain connections being made.
- The primary way that infants and toddlers learn is through play and caring interaction.
- Babies thrive when they are cared for by "people who are crazy about them" (Bronfenbrenner, 1976).

THE RISKS
- The first three years of life need to be filled with safety, loving interactions, and play.
- When children grow up with abuse, chaos, or poor interactions, their brains do not grow to their full potential, and serious behavioral, emotional, educational, or social problems can result.

GROWTH ISSUES
- Remember to hold young infants while they are fed. Look at them, touch them, and talk or sing to them. This helps them use the nutrition they are getting and provides needed stimulation.
- Limit children's use of television; the American Academy of Pediatrics recommends no television for children under the age of two years.
- Name things in your child's environment, identify body parts, and name pictures in books as you read every day. Eventually, you may notice that your child will try to "read" to you!
- Children and older toddlers can learn many skills by being allowed to "help" with tasks such as safe cooking activities, cleaning, and laundry in their own way. Talking to your child about these activities will also increase his or her vocabulary and understanding.
- Allow your child to gain supervised experience with nontoxic art materials such as crayons and playdough; this can help him or her become more creative and develop fine motor skills. Expect that it will take time for your child to be very accurate in using these materials.

FOR MORE INFORMATION
http://www.zerotothree.org/child-development/brain-development

Child Abuse Prevention: Learning about Neglect

THE FACTS

- Child neglect can happen by any person who is responsible for caring for a child: a parent, a child care provider, or a babysitter.
- Neglect is the most common form of child maltreatment and is identified as the cause of death in more than one third of all child maltreatment fatalities. More than 1,500 children die from maltreatment each year in the United States.
- Children can be neglected in many ways:
  - Not being supervised
  - Not being given medical care
  - Not being given adequate food, water, or shelter
  - Not being nurtured appropriately
  - Not being taken to school (if school age)
  - Being raised in a filthy or unsafe environment

THE RISKS

- All of the types of neglect listed above can have serious consequences for children's survival, brain development, and growth.
- Because neglect can be serious, and even fatal, it is required to be reported to state child protective services. If you suspect you know a child who is not being supervised or otherwise cared for, you can call directly or speak to your child's teacher about how to make a report.

WHAT YOU CAN DO

- The most important thing you can do is to supervise your child by sight and sound at all times and, when you cannot be with your child, to choose a caregiver who will do the same.
- Be especially aware of common hazards such as bodies of water, lack of smoke detectors, and unsafe sleeping conditions.
- If you are having trouble meeting your child's basic needs, you can contact child protection directly or contact your child's teacher for a consultation on how to access resources you may need.

FOR MORE INFORMATION

http://www.childwelfare.gov/preventing/preventionmonth/tipsheets.cfm

Motor Vehicle Safety

THE FACTS

- Motor vehicle collisions are the number-one cause of death for all children in the United States.
- Child safety seats reduce the risk of death in passenger cars by 71 percent for infants, and by 54 percent for toddlers up to four years of age.

THE RISKS

- Nearly two-thirds of all children killed in car crashes were driven by a drunk driver.
- Adults who do not wear their own seat belts are less likely to have children buckled in their seats.

WHAT PARENTS CAN DO

- Wear your own seat belt; it sets a good example of safety.
- Remember that children need to be in a rear-facing seat through their second year of life.
- Make sure that children are in appropriate car safety seats based on age, weight, and height.
- Children under the age of 13 years should not sit in the front seat of a vehicle.
- Children shorter than 4 feet 9 inches need to use a booster seat.

FOR MORE INFORMATION

http://www.cdc.gov/MotorVehicleSafety/Child_Passenger_Safety/CPS-Factsheet.html

Fire Safety

THE FACTS
- Almost two-thirds of all fire deaths in the home occurred in homes without a working smoke detector.
- Preschool- and kindergarten-age children are responsible for many fatal fires each year because of playing with matches or lighters. They are very likely to perish in these fires.

SUPERVISION ISSUES
- Make sure that smoke detectors are installed and working. Change the batteries twice a year.
- Find a locked location to store lighters, matches, and other fire starters. Remember that young children will get into purses and bags where these are stored, even if they have been told not to do so.
- Use positive messages and instruction to teach young children about fire safety. Avoid making threats against children; they will naturally be tempted to hide themselves or attempt to hide a fire they have started. This can result in death.
- Educate children about evacuation plans, and practice these plans.

FOR MORE INFORMATION
http://www.nfpa.org

Safe Sleeping

THE FACTS
- Each year, more than 800 infants die from accidental suffocation. This includes any death that chokes, strangles, or smothers a baby.
- Babies who sleep with adults are 20 times more likely to die from suffocation than babies who sleep alone in a crib.

THE RISKS
Sleeping with adults or older siblings; the use of blankets, pillows, and crib bumpers; dangling cords; plastic bags; and unsupervised use of small objects that can be placed in the mouth can all be deadly.

SUPERVISION ISSUES
- Babies younger than one year old should sleep alone in a crib without a crib bumper, blankets, pillows, or stuffed animals.
- Babies should always be put to sleep on their backs, never their bellies or sides.
- Babies can safely sleep in their own beds in their parents' room, if parents desire, for supervision and convenience of breast-feeding or soothing. Babies should not sleep in the same crib with other babies at the same time.

FOR MORE INFORMATION
Information about sudden infant death syndrome (SIDS) and safe sleep: http://www.nichd.nih.gov/publications/pubs/safe_sleep_gen.cfm

Toy Safety

THE FACTS
- Although toys are thought to be safer than ever, many still contain hazards that are not discovered until after they hit the market. Caregivers have to assess the safety of all toys.
- Common toy-related hazards include choking by swallowing objects, having strings or cords wrapped around one's neck, or being smothered by plastic overwraps. Head injuries and electrocution are also possible.

THE RISKS
Children can be injured by toys that are safe for some ages but not for others. For instance, a game marketed for an eight-year-old may contain small parts that could cause a two-year-old to choke.

SUPERVISION ISSUES
- Buy toys that are appropriate for children's developmental ages.
- Children under the age of eight years should not use toys that plug in because of risks associated with burns and electrocution.
- For children who are able to use riding toys, remember to use helmets and other safety gear. Head injuries can occur from a fall, even from a small toy. Also ensure that children never ride near stairs or bodies of water.
- Remove plastic wrappings completely, and ensure that any cord or string attached to a toy is too short to go around a child's neck.

FOR MORE INFORMATION
Handout on how to choose the right toys for children:
http://www.cpsc.gov/cpscpub/pubs/285.pdf.

To receive product recall information, sign up at www.cpsc.gov.

Choosing a Caregiver

Sometimes you will need to select a backup caregiver or a babysitter. Following are some considerations to help you make the best choices for your child. A babysitter should:

- be an adult, not another child.
- have experience or training in caring for children.
- have references who are not related to him or her.
- submit to a background check.
- agree to remain sober while caring for your child.
- be able to discuss what he or she will do in an emergency and be able to follow any written instructions or phone numbers you leave.
- not carry a weapon into your home.
- not take any prescription medication that may make him or her sleepy or confused while caring for your child.
- be patient and calm.
- never shake or hit your baby under any circumstances.
- never withhold food or force food on a child.
- never medicate your child unless instructed to do so, and never give your child alcohol.
- never bring any person into your home or around your child whom you have not approved.

FOR MORE INFORMATION

How to choose a babysitter:
http://kidshealth.org/parent/positive/family/babysitter.html#

Background checks:
http://www.nannypro.com/content/pages/ background-checks
(NOTE: This is only one of a number of paid services; checks can also be completed directly through your state's bureau of investigation. You will likely need written consent for this type of check.)

Dogs and Children

THE FACTS

- Approximately 4.5 million people are bitten each year by dogs in the United States; 400,000 children are bitten so severely that they need medical attention.
- Children are at risk from birth for being bitten, attacked, or killed by a dog . Even gentle dogs who have not been provoked have killed infants as young as two weeks old. There is no way to predict which dogs will attack an infant, or when.

THE RISKS

- Infants can be quickly maimed or killed by dogs, even while supervised.
- Toddlers and older children may not consistently understand how to interact appropriately with dogs and can unintentionally threaten an animal.

SUPERVISION ISSUES

- Never, ever leave an infant alone with a dog, no matter how gentle. Never allow a dog to sleep in the room with an infant.
- Model appropriate behaviors with pets; never approach a dog who is eating, sleeping, or chained, or who appears ill. Talk with children about never touching a dog without permission and never approaching a stray dog.
- Even puppies can fatally attack infants, who are totally helpless. Never underestimate a puppy, and never leave an infant where a puppy can get to him or her.

FOR MORE INFORMATION

Dogs and kids:
http://www.cdc.gov/HomeandRecreationalSafety/Dog-Bites/biteprevention.html

Tips on getting a new dog:
http://www.petco.com/caresheets/dog/Dog_ChildSafety.pdf

Accidental Poisoning

THE FACTS

More than 1.2 million children are accidentally poisoned each year.

THE RISKS

In addition to toxins such as lead paint and carbon monoxide, children are commonly poisoned by medications, cosmetics, and cleaning supplies. Young children eagerly explore handbags, cabinets, and objects on countertops as well as any bottle or jar that they may encounter.

SUPERVISION CHECKLIST

__ All cleaning chemicals and detergents are locked away.

__ All medications are locked in a cabinet out of children's sight.

__ Medication is never left in handbags, briefcases, or diaper bags that may be explored by children.

__ Carbon monoxide detectors are installed in my home.

__ I leave all cleaners in their original packages and never mix them.

__ If my house was built before 1978, I have had it checked for lead paint.

FOR MORE INFORMATION

http://www.safekids.org/safety-basics/safety-spotlight/poison-prevention-week

Poison control hotline: 1-800-222-1222

Water Safety

THE FACTS
Drowning is the leading cause of death by injury for children ages one to four years.

THE RISKS
Children may drown in pools, hot tubs, buckets of water, lakes, ponds, rivers, toilets, bathtubs, decorative fountains, or any other water source. There is no safe way to leave a child alone near water.

SUPERVISION ISSUES
- Never leave a child unattended in or near water. This includes swimming pools, hot tubs, fountains, lakes, ponds, and the ocean.
- When children are near water, ensure that they are wearing appropriate safety vests. These are no substitute for supervision, however.
- Flotation toys are not substitutes for other safety measures.
- Even children who have had swimming lessons should not be left alone.
- Never force a child to drink excessive amounts of water as a punishment. This can lead to water intoxication and can be fatal.
- Ensure that a home pool has a gate around it, and include a lock and alarm.

FOR MORE INFORMATION
http://www.safekids.org/safety-basics/safety-resources-by-risk-area/drowning

Talking with and Listening to Your Child

THE FACTS

- Life is busy, especially for families with young children.
- Children are never as interested in getting our attention as when we are on the phone, in the bathtub, or trying to concentrate on something else.
- Children are learning from what we do as well as what we say.
- Children are always communicating something through their behavior. Sometimes they are overwhelmed, tired, or confused. When we take time to listen and try to see their point of view, we see that there is a reason behind each action. Then we can identify and solve the problem.

THE DISTRACTIONS

- Time uploading photos and describing our lives on Facebook is time we could spend living.
- Children see adults jump into action when the e-mail chimes or the phone beeps. Conversations are often interrupted, and the child cannot remember what he or she wanted to say by the time the adult returns.
- Some schools have banned phone usage in the carpool line because children are being "hushed" when they want to greet their parent and share news of the day.

SUPERVISION ISSUES

- It is difficult to adequately see and hear children when we are distracted by electronic devices.
- Distracted driving accounted for more than 3,000 deaths in 2010. http://www.distraction.gov/content/press-release/2011/12-8.html
- Sometimes children just "want attention." That's OK. They actually need us to talk with and listen to them, so they can learn about the world and develop into healthy and curious kids.

FOR MORE INFORMATION
http://www.pbs.org/parents/talkingwithkids

Playing It Safe at the Park

THE FACTS
- The Consumer Product Safety Commission reports that each year an estimated 51,000 children are treated in U.S. hospital emergency rooms for home playground-related injuries—mostly resulting from falls.
- Climbers and platforms, especially those made from recycled plastic decking, can become very slippery when wet.
- Impact material such as sand, mulch, or pea gravel under swings and climbers should be 12 inches deep and must be replaced when it becomes compacted, gets scattered, or washes away.

THE RISKS
- Young children's skin is thinner and more delicate than the skin of older children and adults. Children have been severely burned by metal and plastic slides, swings, asphalt, concrete, and surface materials such as dark rubber mulch, even on days as mild as 74 degrees.
- Scarves, long necklaces, and drawstrings can catch on slides and climbers and cause strangulation. Do not let children wrap anything around their necks or waists when climbing.
- Openings in guardrails or between ladder rungs that measure less than 3.5 inches or more than 9 inches could trap children's heads, hands, or feet.

SUPERVISION ISSUES
- Very young children have not learned to move away when something burns them. When sitting on something hot, they may not realize where the pain is coming from. Make sure you can see and hear your child at all times. Look for places where heat-reducing coatings have worn off.
- Visually scan the playground for broken equipment, glass, and other debris as you arrive. Do not allow children to play on equipment that is broken or has sharp or jagged edges.
- Check to make sure there is no dangerous hardware such as open *S* hooks or protruding bolt ends.

- Make sure there are no tripping hazards sticking out of the ground.
- Check posted signs for age guidelines. Children often get injured when playing on equipment designed for older or younger children.

FOR MORE INFORMATION
http://www.cpsc.gov/cpscpub/pubs/327.html
http://www.cpsc.gov/CPSCPUB/PUBS/playpubs.html
http://www.safekids.org/safety-basics/safety-resources-by-risk-area/playground

Neglect Issues for the Center or School Handbook

Teachers and directors: Please feel free to use our sample language here to develop prevention-friendly policies for your handbook. You may use this language directly or as a basis to develop your own policies.

Transportation Issues Policy

All children must be restrained in a properly installed child safety seat in order to be picked up from the center, including rear-facing seats for infants, child seats, and/or booster seats according to the child's age, height, and weight. All car seats will be viewed at the time a child is enrolled in the center to ensure compliance with this policy; additionally, center staff reserve the right to inspect a car seat at any time as a routine safety check. Any caregiver who is observed to transport a child without a safety seat will be considered to engage in neglectful behavior, and appropriate authorities will be contacted. Child safety is considered an essential mission of our center, and we will never purposefully permit a child's life to be endangered.

Additionally, any family member or caregiver who presents to the center and is suspected of being impaired will not be permitted to transport a child, and the center reserves the right to contact appropriate authorities. This includes but is not limited to someone who is intoxicated by drugs or alcohol.

Naptime Policy

Although we understand the need for children to have a comfortable rest time with a comfort item, we are mindful that stuffed animals and pillows can be suffocation hazards for infants. Therefore, we do not allow infants to sleep with a pillow or stuffed animal. We also do not use crib bumpers, nor do we encourage their use at home. All infants will be placed on their backs to sleep according to best practices; any exceptions must have a doctor's note on file.

Child Neglect Policy

According to the laws of our state, the employees of our center are all considered "mandated reporters" of child abuse and neglect. That means that if we suspect that a child is being abused or neglected, then we are required to report it. It does not mean that an investigation will occur, but we must bring it to the attention of authorities. The prevention of child maltreatment (abuse and neglect) is a core value for our center, and we work hard to make sure that every child is safe and well. We follow this definition of neglect: "A condition in which a caretaker responsible for the child, either deliberately or by extraordinary inattentiveness, permits the child to experience avoidable present suffering and/or fails to provide one or more of the ingredients generally deemed essential for developing a person's physical, intellectual, and emotional capacities." (Polansky, Hally, & Polansky, 1975).

We generally interpret this to indicate that children can be neglected by not being cared for physically or emotionally, by not being watched carefully enough, or by not being given medical care. While your child is with us, we will provide enriching and developmentally appropriate care that is not neglectful. If you have concerns about how your child is being cared for with us, or if you are unable to meet your child's basic needs, please talk to your teacher or the center director. We can provide a referral for resources such as food or clothing. If we suspect neglect, we will meet with you confidentially about our concerns. This will not excuse us from making a report, but we will attempt to allow you to make the report with us. Child safety is a priority at our center.

Child Abuse Hotlines

National Child Abuse Hotline:
Childhelp 800-422-4453
www.childhelp.org

Alabama
Local (toll): (334) 242-9500
http://tinyurl.com/cldgpq9
State website for information on reporting; child abuse reporting numbers are listed by county, or call Childhelp® (800-422-4453) for assistance.

Alaska
Toll-Free: (800) 478-4444
http://tinyurl.com/bwq2dj8

Arizona
Toll-Free: (888) SOS-CHILD (888-767-2445)
http://tinyurl.com/6p726sm

Arkansas
Toll-Free: (800) 482-5964
http://tinyurl.com/bo9ewlx

California
http://tinyurl.com/3cgjdxw
State website for information on reporting; child abuse reporting numbers are listed by county, or call Childhelp® (800-422-4453) for assistance.

Colorado
Local (toll): (303) 866-5932
http://tinyurl.com/csev7dy
State website for information on reporting; child abuse reporting numbers are listed by county, or call Childhelp® (800-422-4453) for assistance.

Connecticut
TDD: (800) 624-5518
Toll-Free: (800) 842-2288
http://tinyurl.com/y86zjtd

Delaware
Toll-Free: (800) 292-9582
http://tinyurl.com/c5x2ur3

District of Columbia
Local (toll): (202) 671-SAFE (202-671-7233)
http://tinyurl.com/c4wvumk

Florida
Toll-Free: (800) 96-ABUSE (800-962-2873)
http://tinyurl.com/c7hr2pl

Georgia
Local: (404) 651-9361
http://tinyurl.com/blkqjex
State website for information on reporting; child abuse reporting numbers are listed by county, or call Childhelp® (800-422-4453) for assistance.

Hawaii
Local (toll): (808) 832-5300
http://tinyurl.com/crok2ec

Idaho
TDD: (208) 332-7205
Toll-Free: (800) 926-2588
http://tinyurl.com/c6vn3gk

Illinois
Toll-Free: (800) 252-2873
Local (toll): (217) 524-2606
http://tinyurl.com/d7o8p8

Indiana
Toll-Free: (800) 800-5556
http://tinyurl.com/cb8u7ml

Iowa
Toll-Free: (800) 362-2178
http://tinyurl.com/cmxy3x9

Kansas
Toll-Free: (800) 922-5330
http://tinyurl.com/d6rbh32

Kentucky
Toll-Free: (877) 597-2331
http://tinyurl.com/28y7lft

Louisiana
Toll-Free: (855) 452-5437
http://tinyurl.com/cfdesog

Maine
TDD: (800) 963-9490
Toll-Free: (800) 452-1999
http://tinyurl.com/c5rufnv

Maryland
http://tinyurl.com/cjgonxh
State website for information on reporting;
child abuse reporting numbers are listed by
county, or call Childhelp® (800-422-4453) for
assistance.

Massachusetts
Toll-Free: (800) 792-5200
http://tinyurl.com/chhe5ba

Michigan
Toll-Free: (800) 942-4357
Local: (855) 444-3911
http://tinyurl.com/d62lh9b

Minnesota
http://tinyurl.com/28bmuv
State website for information on reporting;
child abuse reporting numbers are listed by
county, or call Childhelp® (800-422-4453) for
assistance.

Mississippi
Toll-Free: (800) 222-8000
Local (toll): (601) 359-4991
http://tinyurl.com/88tkefw

Missouri
Toll-Free: (800) 392-3738
Local: (573) 751-3448
http://tinyurl.com/6p4xsp2

Montana
Toll-Free: (866) 820-5437
http://tinyurl.com/8a6qevj

Nebraska
Toll-Free: (800) 652-1999
http://tinyurl.com/7mjjna6

Nevada
Toll-Free: (800) 992-5757
Local: (775) 684-4400
http://tinyurl.com/chy2hl9

New Hampshire
Toll-Free: (800) 894-5533
Local (toll): (603) 271-6556
http://tinyurl.com/cg2s5vh

New Jersey
TDD: (800) 835-5510
Toll-Free: (877) 652-2873
http://tinyurl.com/dxu98d6

New Mexico
Toll-Free: (855) 333-7233
http://tinyurl.com/cvxvsgg

New York
TDD: (800) 369-2437
Toll-Free: (800) 342-3720
Local (toll): (518) 474-8740
http://tinyurl.com/4nt4b9s

North Carolina
http://tinyurl.com/bt43hfw
State website for information on reporting;
child abuse reporting numbers are listed by
county, or call Childhelp® (800-422-4453) for
assistance.

North Dakota
http://tinyurl.com/cgdln4m
State website for information on reporting;
child abuse reporting numbers are listed by
county, or call Childhelp® (800-422-4453) for
assistance.

Ohio
Phone: (800) 422-4453
http://tinyurl.com/3wa2mvh
Contact the county public children services
agency using the information above or call
Childhelp® (800-422-4453) for assistance.

Oklahoma
Toll-Free: (800) 522-3511
http://tinyurl.com/853fwcj

Oregon
http://tinyurl.com/23p2pat
State website for information on reporting;
child abuse reporting numbers are listed by
county, or call Childhelp® (800-422-4453) for
assistance.

Pennsylvania
TDD: (866) 872-1677
Toll-Free: (800) 932-0313
http://tinyurl.com/23p2pat

Puerto Rico
Toll-Free: (800) 981-8333
Local (toll): (787) 749-1333

Rhode Island
Toll-Free: (800) RI-CHILD (800-742-4453)
http://tinyurl.com/bsk4tor

South Carolina
Local (toll): (803) 898-7318
http://tinyurl.com/bu4edhm
State website for information on reporting;
child abuse reporting numbers are listed by
county, or call Childhelp® (800-422-4453) for
assistance.

South Dakota
Phone: (605) 773-3227
Toll-Free: (866) 847-7335
http://tinyurl.com/bsp4xvc
State website for information on reporting;
child abuse reporting numbers are listed by
county, or call Childhelp® (800-422-4453) for
assistance.

Tennessee
Toll-Free: (877) 237-0004
http://tinyurl.com/8xerdl7
http://tinyurl.com/dxcgty3

Texas
Department of Family and Protective
Services
Toll-Free: (800) 252-5400
http://tinyurl.com/cdyvo3r
Spanish: http://tinyurl.com/boyjsee

Utah
Local: (855) 323-3237
Toll-Free: (800) 678-9399
http://tinyurl.com/bpjltoe

Vermont
After hours: (800) 649-5285
http://tinyurl.com/bvr7r8w

Virginia
Toll-Free: (800) 552-7096
Local (toll): (804) 786-8536
http://tinyurl.com/d9dn26d

Washington
TDD: (800) 624-6186
Toll-Free: (800) 562-5624
(866) END-HARM (866-363-4276)
http://tinyurl.com/mw2tkg

West Virginia
Toll-Free: (800) 352-6513
http://tinyurl.com/hzd7m

Wisconsin
http://tinyurl.com/css5bk7
State website for information on reporting;
child abuse reporting numbers are listed by
county, or call Childhelp® (800-422-4453) for
assistance.

Wyoming
http://tinyurl.com/bwrqmk5
State website for information on reporting;
child abuse reporting numbers are listed by
county, or call Childhelp® (800-422-4453) for
assistance.

Child Maltreatment Resources

Resources for Teachers

Committee for Children: Resources include curriculum on the prevention of bullying, youth violence, child abuse, and family education. Training and technical assistance available.
Address: 2815 Second Ave., Suite 400
Seattle, WA 98121
Phone: (800) 634-4449 ext. 6223
Fax: (206) 438-6765
www.cfchildren.org

Education Resources Information Center (ERIC): Access to a large body of education-related resources. Database contains more than one million records.
Address: ERIC Program c/o CSC
655 15th St. NW, Suite 500,
Washington, DC 2005
Phone: (800) LET-ERIC
www.eric.ed.gov

National Association for the Education of Young Children (NAEYC): Provides training, resources, conferences, and position statements to help educators and early childhood professionals care for and protect young children.
Address: 1313 L St NW, Suite 500
Washington, DC 20005
Phone: (202) 232-8777
Toll-Free: (800) 424-2460
www.naeyc.org

National Child Traumatic Stress Network: Provides resources, training, and services to educators, families, and children to improve access to help for children who are experiencing traumatic stress.
Address: 11150 W. Olympic Blvd., Suite 650
Los Angeles, CA 90064
Phone: (310) 235-2633
Fax: (310) 235-2612
www.nctsn.org

National Education Association: Promotes quality public education and professional advances in education. Information, grant opportunities, and professional development opportunities available.
Address: 1201 16th St. NW
Washington, DC 20036
Phone: (202) 833-4000
Fax: (202) 822-7974
www.nea.org

School Social Work Association of America: Encourages the professional development of school social workers to enhance the educational experience of students and their families.
Address: P.O. Box 1086
Sumner, WA 98390
Phone: (847) 289-4527
www.sswaa.org

Resources for the Public

Childhelp: Provides counseling for adult abuse survivors and child victims of abuse. Also provides counseling opportunities for abuse offenders and parents, and operates a national hotline.
Address: 15757 N. 78th St.
Scottsdale, AZ 85260
Phone: (800) 4-A-CHILD
        (800) 2-A-CHILD (TDD)
        (480) 922-7061
Fax: (480) 922-7061
www.childhelpusa.org

National Center for Missing and Exploited Children: Offers assistance to parents, law enforcement, schools, and community organizations in recovering missing children. Provides ongoing public awareness about ways to prevent child abduction, molestation, and exploitation.
Address: Charles B. Wang International Children's Building
699 Prince St.
Alexandria, VA 22314
Phone: (800) 843-5678
        (703) 224-2150

Fax: (703) 274-2122
www.missingkids.com

Parents Anonymous: Support groups to help parents provide caring, nurturing home environments.
Address: 981 Corporate Center Dr., Suite 100
Pomona, CA 91768
Phone: (909) 236-5757
Fax: (909) 236-5758
www.parentsanonymous.org

Parents Helping Parents: Strives to improve the quality of life for all children through educating, supporting, and training their parents and primary caregivers.
Address: Sobrato Center for Nonprofits—San Jose
1400 Parkmoor Ave., Suite 100
San Jose, CA 95126
Phone: (408) 727-5775
        (855) 727-5775
Fax: (408) 286-1116
www.php.com

National Fatherhood Initiative: Provides support for fathers and works to improve the well-being of children by increasing the number of children growing up with committed fathers.
Address: 20410 Observation Dr., Suite 107
Germantown, MD 20876
Phone: (301) 948-0599
Fax: (301) 948-6776
www.fatherhood.org

Prevention Organizations

Child Abuse Prevention Association: Provides prevention and treatment services to the children and families of abuse. Helps families deal with the stress of a traumatic event and begin to heal. Helps train families to create strong and healthy home environments.
Address: 503 E. 23rd St.
Independence, MO 64055
Phone: (816) 252-8388
Fax: (816) 252-1337
www.childabuseprevention.org

International Society for Prevention of Child Abuse and Neglect (ISPCAN): Provides information, trainings, and statistics to help support individuals and organizations working to protect children from abuse and neglect.
Address: 13123 E. 16th Ave., Suite B390
Aurora, CO 80045
Phone: (303) 864-5220
Fax: (303) 864-5222
www.ispcan.org

National Alliance of Children's Trust and Prevention Funds: Assists state children's trust and prevention funds to strengthen families and protect children.
Address: P.O. Box 15206
Seattle, WA 98115
Phone: (517) 432-5096
Fax: (517) 432-2476
www.ctfalliance.org

National Center on Shaken Baby Syndrome: Provides resources and information designed to prevent shaken baby syndrome and other forms of physical child abuse. Provides education to increase positive parenting and child care.
Address: 1433 N. Highway 89, Suite 110
Farmington, UT 84025
Phone: (801) 447-9364
www.dontshake.org

National Exchange Club Foundation for the Prevention of Child Abuse: Provides education, intervention, and support to families affected by child abuse and launches local campaigns to prevent and fight against child abuse.
Address: 3050 Central Ave.
Toledo, OH 43606
Phone: (800) 924-2643
(419) 535-3232
Fax: (419) 535-1989
http://preventchildabuse.com

Prevent Child Abuse America: Provides education and hope through inspirational stories to prevent abuse and neglect. Helps strengthen families and encourage communities.
Address: 228 S. Wabash Ave., 10th Floor
Chicago, IL 60604
Phone: (312) 663-3520
(800) CHILDREN
Fax: (312) 939-8962
www.preventchildabuse.org

U.S. Department of Health and Human Services: Provides resources on child abuse prevention, protecting children from abuse, and strengthening families, as well as individual state statutes and reporting laws.
Address: Child Welfare Information Gateway
Children's Bureau/ACYF
1250 Maryland Ave. SW, 8th Floor
Washington, DC 20024
Phone: (800) 394-3366
www.childwelfare.gov/preventing

Child Welfare Organizations

American Humane Association Children's Division: Research agency that provides analysis, training, and ongoing research to help agencies respond to child abuse.
Address: 1400 16th St. NW, Suite 360
Washington DC 20036
Phone: (800) 227-4645
(303) 792-9900
Fax: (303) 792-5333
www.americanhumane.org

American Professional Society on the Abuse of Children: Provides professional education, helps advocate for current research and effective practice in the child maltreatment field, and addresses public policy issues.
Address: 350 Poplar Ave.
Elmhurst, IL 60126
Phone: (630) 941-1235
(877) 402-7722
Fax: (630) 359-4272
www.apsac.org

American Public Human Services Association: Resources include program and policy issues related to the administration and awarding of publicly funded human services.
Address: 1133 19th St. NW, Suite 400
Washington, DC 20036
Phone: (202) 682-0100
Fax: (202) 289-6555
www.aphsa.org

AVANCE Family Support and Education Program: National training center that provides information, materials, and curriculum to providers helping support high-risk Hispanic families.
Address: 118 N. Medina St.
San Antonio, TX 78207
Phone: (210) 270-4630
Fax: (210) 270-4636
www.avance.org

Child Welfare League of America: Provides training and technical assistance to child welfare personnel and agencies. Educates the public and professionals about ongoing issues affecting children.
Address: 1726 M St. NW, Suite 500
Washington, DC 20036
Phone: (202) 688-4200
Fax: (202) 833-1689
Web address: www.cwla.org

National Black Child Development Institute: Holds a national training conference in collaboration with Howard University to improve the lives of and protect African American children.
Address: 1313 L. St. NW, Suite 110
Washington, DC 20005
Phone: (202) 833-2220
Fax: (202) 833-8222
www.nbcdi.org

National Indian Child Welfare Association: Provides assistance and information on Native American child welfare issues. Supports communities in development and advocacy surrounding the needs of Native American children. Supports efforts to facilitate tribal responses to the needs of Native American families and children.
Address: 5100 S.E. Macadam Ave., Suite 300
Portland, OR 97201
Phone: (503) 222-4004
Fax: (503) 222-4007
www.nicwa.org

National Resource Center on Child Maltreatment: Helps states, tribes, and local agencies develop successful child protective services. A collaboration between Action for Child Protection and Child Welfare Institute goals flexes to meet the current needs in prevention, identification, and treatment of child abuse.
Address: 2494 S. Sedalia Circle
Aurora, CO 80013
Phone: (518) 767-0182
Fax: (303) 369-8009
www.gocwi.org

Child Advocacy Organizations

Children's Defense Fund: Provides research and education opportunities, and helps campaign to improve policies and programs for children. Advocates to change laws and helps fight and prevent abuse.
Address: 25 E. St. NW
Washington, DC 20001
Phone: (800) CDF-1200
www.childrensdefense.org

Court Appointed Special Advocates (CASA): Supports local and national court-appointed volunteer advocacy, so that every abused or neglected child is safe and has an opportunity to thrive.
Address: National CASA Association
100 W. Harrison St., North Tower, Suite 500
Seattle, WA 98119
www.iamforthechild.org

National Children's Advocacy Center: Provides training on prevention, intervention, and treatment services to abused children and their families with a child-centered team approach.
Address: 210 Pratt Ave.
Huntsville, AL 35801
Phone: (256) 533-KIDS
Fax: (256) 534-6883
www.nationalcac.org

Voices for America's Children: Child advocacy organization providing information, research, and network opportunities on multiple child issues, including child maltreatment.
Address: 1000 Vermont Ave. NW, Suite 700
Washington, DC 20005
Phone: (202) 289-0777
www.voices.org

Zero to Three National Center for Infants, Toddlers, and Families: A national nonprofit organization that informs, trains, and supports professionals, policy makers, and parents in their efforts to improve the lives of infants and toddlers.
Address: 1255 23rd St., NW, Suite 350
Washington, DC 20037
Phone: (202) 638-1144
Fax: (202) 638-0851
www.zerotothree.org

Children's Book Index

All the Places to Love by Patricia MacLachlan, 63

The Carrot Seed by Ruth Krauss, 64

Chrysanthemum by Kevin Henkes, 64

The Crayon Box That Talked by Shane DeRolf, 63

Do You Want to Be My Friend? by Eric Carle, 63

Draw Me a Star by Eric Carle, 62

Fish Is Fish by Leo Lionni, 64

Goodnight Moon by Margaret Wise Brown, 62

Grandfather Twilight by Barbara Berger, 62

The Grapes of Wrath by John Steinbeck, 13

Hug by Jez Alborough, 62

I Love My Hair! by Natasha Anastasia Tarpley, 64

Jamaica Tag-Along by Juanita Havill, 64

The Kissing Hand by Audrey Penn, 63

The Lamb and the Butterfly by Arnold Sundgaard, 64

Leo the Late Bloomer by Robert Kraus, 64

The Little Match Girl by Hans Christian Andersen, 13

The Maggie B by Irene Haas, 64

The Magic Hat by Mem Fox, 63

Mama, Do You Love Me? by Barbara M. Joosse, 63

The Rainbow Fish by Marcus Pfister, 64

The Royal Raven by Hans Wilhelm, 64

Sheila Rae, the Brave by Kevin Henkes, 64

Snuggle Puppy by Sandra Boynton, 62

Tacky the Penguin by Helen Lester, 64

Tell Me a Story, Mama by Angela Johnson, 62

Time for Bed by Mem Fox, 62

Today I Feel Silly and Other Moods That Make My Day by Jamie Lee
   Curtis, 62

Uncle Jed's Barbershop by Margaree King Mitchell, 64

The Very Quiet Cricket by Eric Carle, 63

Wemberly Worried by Kevin Henkes, 62

What a Wonderful World by George David Weiss, 63

What Comes in Spring? by Barbara Savadge Horton, 62

When I Was Little: A Four-Year-Old's Memoirs of Her Youth by Jamie Lee
   Curtis, 63

Wilfrid Gordon McDonald Partridge by Mem Fox, 64

Index

A

Abandonment, 27
Abuse, 6, 35, 58, 92-93, 100
Accidents, 15, 25-26
Accommodating therapies, 56-57, 66
Active listening, 56, 110
Acute neglect, 14-18, 21-22, 36-38, 44
Age as risk factor, 24-25, 32, 73
Aggression, 6, 17, 35, 51
American Academy of Pediatrics, 15, 20, 75
American Humane Association Children's
    Division, 122
American Professional Society on the Abuse of
    Children, 122
American Psychological Association, 20, 75
American Public Human Services
    Association, 123
Asphyxiation, 26
Attachment, 17, 58
Attention problems, 17
AVANCE Family Support and Education
    Program, 123
Avoidance, 35

B

Baby Doe, 29
Babysitters, 14, 22, 34, 106
Bathtub safety, 26-27, 30, 109
Behavioral problems, 20, 100
Bibliotherapy, 61-64, 67
Books, 55
Bullying, 61

C

Car seats, 29, 80, 102, 113
Case studies, 81-95
    deprivation on needs neglect, 82-85, 88-89
    educational neglect, 88-89
    emotional neglect, 82-83, 90-93
    environmental neglect, 84-85, 88-89
    medical neglect, 94-95
    supervisory neglect, 86-87
Center/school handbook, 113-114
    child neglect policy, 114
    naptime, 114
    transportation, 113
Child Abuse Prevention and Treatment Act
    (CAPTA), 13, 78
    Reauthorization Act, 13, 15, 75
Child Abuse Prevention Association, 121

Child abuse prevention hotlines, 11, 45, 115-117
Child advocacy, 69-71
    organizations, 124
Child care providers, 9-10, 14, 16, 22, 28, 106
Child Death Review Board, 23-24, 26, 32
Child development, 47, 66, 100
Child protective services, 24, 32, 45-47, 50
Child Welfare Information Gateway, 19, 50
Child Welfare League of America, 123
Child welfare organizations, 122-123
Childhelp, 75, 120
Children with special needs, 57
Children's Defense Fund, 124
Choking, 26, 105
Chronic neglect, 14-18, 21-22, 36-38, 44
Committee for Children, 119
Community resources, 59-60, 66, 79-80
Community standards, 39-41, 43
Compliance, 34
Confidentiality, 10, 36, 94-95
Consumer Product Safety Commission, 111
Co-sleeping, 26, 32, 104
Court Appointed Special Advocates, 124
Crib safety, 26, 104, 114
Cross-cultural training, 58
Cultural values, 39-41, 43, 55, 58

D

Death certificates, 24
Defiance, 34
Dehydration, 27, 30
Department of Transportation's National
    Highway Safety Administration, 75
Depression, 6, 17, 19, 20, 22, 90-91
Deprivation of needs neglect, 14, 18, 21-22, 27,
    65, 79, 82-85, 88-89, 101
Developmental delays, 34-35, 43, 48
Developmentally appropriate practices, 70
Documentation, 35-36
Dogs and children, 9, 107
Domestic violence, 19
Drowning, 15, 17, 26-27, 30-32, 73, 109
Duty to report, 33-51, 67

E

Eating disorders, 31
Education Resources Information Center, 119
Educational neglect, 16-18, 21-22, 34, 65, 80, 88-
    89, 101
Emotional development, 60-61, 100

Emotional neglect, 17-18, 21-22, 27, 34, 65, 80, 82-83, 90-93, 101
Environmental neglect, 16, 18, 21-22, 27-28, 65, 80, 84-85, 88-89, 101
Establishing suspicion, 33-44
    handling disclosure, 42
    red flags, 33-36
Ethnic minority groups, 20, 58

F
Failure to thrive, 21, 27
Falls, 26
Family history, 20
Fatal neglect, 9, 21-32, 73
    child developmental characteristics, 30-31
    identifying, 23-24
    prevalence, 23
    risk factors, 24-25
    types of, 26-31
Federal guidelines, 13
Fires, 27-28, 30-32, 103

H
Handouts, 10, 54-55, 66, 99-112
Head injuries, 26, 29, 105
Helplessness, 35, 51
Hoarding food, 34
Home visitation, 55, 66-67
Hospital records, 24
Household composition, 24-25
    adoptive parents, 24-25
    foster parents, 10, 24-25
    single parents, 20, 24-25, 32, 47
    step-parents, 24-25
    unrelated adults, 24-25, 32, 48
Humiliation, 18

I
Inappropriate behavior, 34
International Society for Prevention of Child Abuse and Neglect, 121
Isolation, 19, 21

L
Learning problems, 35
Levels of neglect, 36-38

M
Malnutrition, 27, 30-31, 36, 65
Medicaid, 20
Medical examiners, 24, 32
Medical neglect, 13, 15, 18, 21-22, 27-29, 32, 34, 37, 39, 65, 79, 94-95, 101
Memory problems, 25
Mild neglect, 36-37, 43
Modeling, 53, 56, 61, 66-67, 70, 74, 107
Moderate neglect, 36-38, 43
Motor vehicle collisions, 29-31, 37, 102

N
National Alliance of Children's Trust and Prevention Funds, 121
National Association for the Education of Young Children, 9, 45, 77, 119
National Black Child Development Institute, 123
National Center for Educational Statistics, 58, 77
National Center for Missing and Exploited Children, 120
National Center on Shaken Baby Syndrome, 121
National Child Traumatic Stress Network, 119
National Children's Advocacy Center, 77, 124
National Education Association, 119
National Exchange Club Foundation for the Prevention of Child Abuse, 122
National Fatherhood Initiative, 121
National Indian Child Welfare Association, 123
National Resource Center on Child Maltreatment, 123
Neglect, 6, 9,19-23, 39-40, 53-67, 114
    assessing levels, 36-38
    behavioral symptoms, 34
    defining, 13-22
    educational signs, 35
    in the classroom, 10
    pervasiveness, 9-10, 23, 73
    physical signs, 34-35
    red flags, 33-36
    social signs, 35-36
    types of, 14-18
Nurturing, 58
Nutrition, 14, 69, 74

O
Open-ended questions, 42
Overheating, 30

P
Parent handbooks, 10, 46, 54, 66
Parent library, 55, 66
Parent meetings/trainings, 54, 56, 66
Parents, 14, 22, 71
    educating, 37, 67, 69-71
    empowering, 59

Index

handouts for, 10, 54-55, 66, 99-112
prevention/intervention strategies, 53-57
resources for, 120-121
support systems, 47, 66
Parents Anonymous, 120
Parents Helping Parents, 120
Passivity, 35
Patterns, 36
Pets, 26, 80
Physical abuse, 13, 16, 21-22, 23, 32
Playground safety, 111
Poisoning, 30, 32, 108
Police, 24, 32
Pool safety, 26-27
Poverty, 13, 19-20, 32
Prevent Child Abuse America, 122
Prevention/intervention, 53-67, 101
    classroom strategies, 60-65
    organizations, 121-122
    self-assessment, 66-67, 79-80
    strategies for teachers, 57-60

R

Rejection, 34, 90-91
Reporting neglect, 17-18, 45-51, 55, 66
    laws, 50
    sample form, 97-98
    teacher fears, 46-47
    what you need, 47-48
    whose job? 50
Resource referrals, 55
Retaliation, 46
Risk factors, 19-25
Risk taking, 31
Road rage, 29
Routines, 60, 65

S

Safe Kids USA, 26, 77
Scalding, 31
Scapegoating, 18
School failure, 6, 35, 100
School Social Work Association of America, 120
Self-assessment, 10
    establishing suspicion, 40-41, 43-44
    fatal neglect, 32
    prevention/intervention efforts, 79-80
    reporting neglect, 51
    types of neglect, 22
    values and neglect, 40-41

Self-reliance, 61
Severe neglect, 36-38, 43, 86-87
Sexual abuse, 13, 23, 32
Should have known standard, 33, 43
Smothering, 26, 105
Social networks, 19, 21
Social problems, 17, 35-36, 61, 100
Staff development training, 57-58
Stealing, 34, 43
Stress, 20, 35, 56-57
Substance abuse, 6, 15, 17, 19, 22, 25, 28-29, 31,
    34, 36-37, 39, 48, 80, 82-83, 102
Sudden infant death syndrome, 30, 104
Suffocation, 30, 104, 114
Suicide, 29, 31
Sunburn, 111
Supervisory neglect, 15, 17, 21-22, 25-28, 30, 54,
    65, 73, 80, 86-87, 101, 105
Support systems, 47, 66

T

Teachers, 10, 14, 33-44, 46-47, 57-65
    assessing neglect levels, 36-38
    child maltreatment resources, 119-120
    duty to report, 46-47, 50
    handling disclosure, 42
    helping parents, 53-57
    reporting neglect, 45-51
    resources for, 119-120
Tearfulness, 35
Teasing, 61
Toy safety, 105
Traumatic brain injury, 26
Treatable diseases, 30-31

U

U.S. Department of Health and Human Services,
    13, 23, 78, 122
Unintentional injury, 25
Unpredictability, 17, 20, 22, 60

V

Voices for America's Children, 69, 78, 124

W

Water safety, 15, 17, 26-27, 30-32, 73, 109
Weapons, 15, 17-18, 22, 48

Z

Zero to Three National Center for Infants,
    Toddlers, and Families, 124